Quick & Easy
Fish

p

Contents

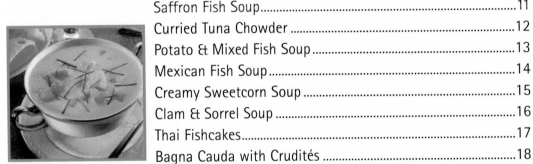

Introduction 4

Fennel, Tomato & Prawn Soup 6

Seafood Chowder 7

Smoked Haddock Soup 8

Salmon & Leek Soup 9

Breton Fish Soup with Cider 10

Saffron Fish Soup 11

Curried Tuna Chowder 12

Potato & Mixed Fish Soup 13

Mexican Fish Soup 14

Creamy Sweetcorn Soup 15

Clam & Sorrel Soup 16

Thai Fishcakes 17

Bagna Cauda with Crudités 18

Smoked Mackerel Pâté 19

Gravadlax 20

Thai-style Crab Sandwich 21

Steamed Yellow Fish Fillets 22

Sesame & Coriander Noodles 23

Hot-smoked Salmon Scramble 24

Cullen Skink 25

Basque Tuna Stew 26

Barbecued Monkfish 27

Swordfish or Tuna Fajitas 28

Tuna Fishcakes 29

Sardines with Pesto 30

Salmon Frittata 31

Mixed Seafood Brochettes 32

Chargrilled Scallops 33

Prawn Rostis 34

Tagliatelle with Broccoli 35

Pasta Puttanesca 36

Seafood Lasagne 37

Spaghettini with Crab 38

Thai Noodles 39

Kedgeree..40

A Modern Kedgeree..41

Jambalaya 42

Prawn & Asparagus Risotto..............................43

Coconut Rice with Monkfish.............................44

Moules Marinières...45

Baked Cod with Curry.....................................46

Fried Fish with Soy Sauce................................47

Tuna in Sweet-&-Sour Sauce 48

Thai-spiced Salmon..49

Scallops with Lime & Chilli 50

Goan Fish Curry...51

Mackerel Escabeche..52

Haddock Baked in Yogurt.................................53

Cod Italienne...54

Cotriade 55

Moroccan Fish Tagine 56

Spicy Prawns with Courgettes...........................57

Poached Rainbow Trout....................................58

Hake Steaks with Chermoula............................59

Stuffed Mackerel 60

Skate with Black Butter....................................61

Dover Sole à la Meunière.................................62

Sea Bass with Ratatouille 63

Whole Sea Bass with Ginger............................64

Stuffed Monkfish Tail......................................65

Seared Tuna Steaks..66

Swordfish à la Maltaise....................................67

Wrapped Red Mullet 68

Plaice Fillets with Grapes.................................69

Potato-topped Cod...70

Warm Tuna Salad..71

Smoked Haddock Salad 72

Lime- & Basil-cured Salmon............................73

Caesar Salad..74

Skate & Spinach Salad.....................................75

Salpicon of Crab 76

Salade Niçoise 77

Lobster & Lime Salad 78

Sweet-&-Sour Fish Salad..................................79

Introduction

Seafood deserves its image as a healthy food. It is rich in protein, and oily fish, such as mackerel and herring, are high in polyunsaturated fats (the type that helps reduce cholesterol levels). White fish are a good source of minerals as well as low in fat, especially if poached, steamed, or lightly grilled. Shellfish have been linked with high cholesterol, but they are also low in saturated fats and it is therefore healthy to eat them in moderation. The variety of fish and shellfish is staggering. You could eat seafood just once a week for a year without having the same dish twice. Seafood is quick and easy to prepare, making it an attractive ingredient for the busy cook. Many types of fish and most shellfish are sold ready to cook and so can be prepared in minutes. Fish is very good value for money by comparison with meat as there is much less waste and no fat or gristle to contend with. Making fish a regular part of your diet therefore makes a lot of sense.

Buying Fish and Shellfish

Wherever you shop for fish, at your trusted local fishmonger or at a supermarket, these guidelines apply:

- The eyes of the fish should be clear, bright and moist. Fish with dull, grey or cloudy eyes should be avoided.
- The gills should be bright red or pink, not dull or grey.
- Fish should smell of the sea and nothing else. Cooked shellfish should smell fresh, with no hint of ammonia.
- If you press the fish lightly with your thumb, the flesh should spring back, leaving little or no imprint.
- The shells of hinged shellfish, such as oysters, mussels and clams, should be tightly closed before cooking. If they are slightly open, tap them sharply. If they do not close, discard them.

Storing

As you never know when fish was caught, especially if you shop in a supermarket, it is best to cook it on the day you buy it. If you are not planning to eat it straight away, put it in the refrigerator and don't keep it for more than a day or two. Refrigerators are not ideal places to store fish as they tend to have a temperature of about 38°F/5°C and fish is best kept at 32°F/0°C. Put the fish into a plastic container and scatter it with ice. Cover with cling film and store it in the coldest part of the refrigerator.

Firm-fleshed fish, such as turbot, monkfish, and Dover sole, freeze better than sea bass, plaice, and lemon sole, but all deteriorate relatively quickly. Oily fish freezes least successfully, but if you need to keep it for more than two days, freezing is the best option. Thaw it thoroughly and slowly before cooking.

Preparation

The amount of preparation your fish needs depends on where you buy it. Supermarkets may have a wet fish counter with a trained fishmonger on hand, while other suppliers sell their fish vacuum-packed. Many fish are sold already scaled and gutted, and are often available either whole or filleted. A fishmonger will usually do the preparation for you, for a small charge. It is cheaper, however, to buy a whole fish and prepare it yourself. It is not difficult to do and just takes practice.

Equipment

You need little special equipment for the recipes in this book, but if you are inspired by the dishes and plan to cook more fish, any of the following may prove a worthwhile purchase. If you want

to poach whole fish, a fish kettle would be a wise investment. This is an oblong, stainless-steel pan with a lifter and a lid, available in several sizes.

A wok - a Chinese pan with a rounded base - is useful for frying and stir-frying. For deep-frying you will need a deep-frying basket, a large frying pan, and a thermometer. If you like to steam fish, think about buying a double boiler, a bamboo steamer or an electric steamer. If you intend to clean fish yourself, a good filleting knife is an essential tool. Tweezers are also useful for removing small bones.

Different cooking methods suit different fish but, as a general rule, poaching, steaming and stewing tend to produce a more moist result than grilling, baking or barbecuing. Drying out can be minimized, however, if the latter three methods are used at sufficiently high temperatures (reducing moisture loss by ensuring the fish is cooked very quickly).

Poaching

The fish is immersed in a poaching liquid, which might be a court-bouillon, fish stock, milk, beer or cider. To poach successfully, bring the liquid to the boil and as soon as it boils, remove the pan from the heat and leave the fish to finish cooking in the residual warmth. This method helps to prevent overcooking and is also excellent if you want to serve the fish cold.

Steaming

Fish and shellfish benefit from being steamed. A flavoured liquid can be used to steam, which will impart some flavour to the fish as it is being cooked. Steaming is especially good for keeping fish moist and the flavour delicate. It can be done in a fish kettle, a double boiler or in a steamer inserted over a pan of boiling water.

Stewing

Whole fish or smaller pieces can be cooked in liquid along with other ingredients, such as vegetables, as a stew. The fish flavours the liquid as it cooks, producing a distinctive taste.

Grilling

This is one of the quickest and easiest cooking methods for whole fish, steaks and fillets. Shellfish can also be grilled, but may need halving lengthways. For all these, the broiler must be on its highest setting and the fish cooked as close to the heat source as possible.

A barbecue is also very useful for cooking fish. Brush the fish with butter, oil or a marinade before and during cooking to ensure that the flesh remains moist.

Baking and Roasting

This covers all methods of cooking in the oven, including open roasting, casseroling and en papillote. This is a good method to choose for entertaining, because once the dish is in the oven, you are free to prepare other dishes.

Deep-frying

The fish may be coated in batter, flour or breadcrumbs and deep-fried in oil. You need a large, heavy-based saucepan or a deep-fat fryer. Large pieces of fish in batter are best cooked at a temperature of 350°F/180°C, which allows the fish to cook without burning the batter. Fish pieces, such as goujons in breadcrumbs, should be cooked at 190°C/375°F. Drain deep-fried items well on kitchen paper so they remain crisp.

Shallow-frying or Pan-frying

This is a quick method for cooking fish and shellfish, and can take as little as 3–4 minutes. A shallow layer of oil or butter and oil is heated in a frying pan, then the fish is added and cooked until just tender and lightly browned. A good non-stick frying pan is essential.

KEY	
	Simplicity level 1 – 3 (1 easiest, 3 slightly harder)
	Preparation time
	Cooking time

Fennel, Tomato & Prawn Soup

This light and refreshing soup is also good served cold. An ideal starter for a summer meal, served with crunchy melba toast.

NUTRITIONAL INFORMATION

Calories	110	Sugars	.........8g
Protein	........10g	Fat	...........2g
Carbohydrate	...13g	Saturates	.......0g

 10–15 mins   40 mins

SERVES 4

INGREDIENTS

2 tsp olive oil

1 large onion, halved and sliced

2 large fennel bulbs, halved and sliced

1 small potato, diced

850 ml/1½ pints water

400 ml/14 fl oz tomato juice

1 bay leaf

125 g/4½ oz cooked peeled small prawns

2 tomatoes, skinned, deseeded
  and chopped

½ tsp snipped fresh dill

salt and pepper

dill sprigs or fennel fronds, to garnish

melba toast, to serve

1 Heat the olive oil in a large saucepan over a medium heat. Add the onion and fennel and cook for 3–4 minutes, stirring occasionally, until the onion is just softened.

2 Add the potato, water, tomato juice and bay leaf with a large pinch of salt. Reduce the heat, cover and simmer for about 25 minutes, stirring once or twice, until the vegetables are soft.

3 Allow the soup to cool slightly, then transfer to a blender or food processor and purée until smooth, working in batches if necessary. (If using a food processor, strain off the cooking liquid and reserve. Purée the soup solids with enough cooking liquid to moisten them, then combine with the remaining liquid.)

4 Return the soup to the saucepan and add the prawns. Simmer gently for about 10 minutes, to reheat the soup and allow it to absorb the prawn flavour.

5 Stir in the tomatoes and dill. Taste and adjust the seasoning, adding salt, if needed, and pepper. Thin the soup with a little more tomato juice, if wished. Ladle into warm bowls, garnish with dill or fennel fronds and serve with melba toast.

Seafood Chowder

Mussels, an economical choice at the fishmonger, give essential flavour to this soup. The proportions of fish and prawns are flexible.

NUTRITIONAL INFORMATION

Calories	449	Sugars	.........4g
Protein	........34g	Fat	........27g
Carbohydrate	...18g	Saturates	......16g

30 mins | 40 mins

SERVES 6

INGREDIENTS

1 kg/2 lb 4 oz mussels

4 tbsp plain flour

1.5 litres/2¾ pints fish stock

1 tbsp butter

1 large onion, finely chopped

350 g/12 oz skinless white fish fillets, such as cod, sole or haddock

200 g/7 oz cooked or raw peeled prawns

300 ml/10 fl oz whipping cream or double cream

salt and pepper

snipped fresh dill, to garnish

1 Discard any broken mussels and those with open shells. Rinse, pull off any 'beards', and if there are barnacles, scrape them off with a knife under cold running water. Put the mussels in a large, heavy-based saucepan. Cover tightly and cook over a high heat for about 4 minutes, or until the mussels open, shaking the pan occasionally. Remove the mussels from their shells, adding any juices to the cooking liquid. Strain this through a muslin-lined sieve and reserve.

2 Put the flour in a mixing bowl and very slowly whisk in enough of the stock to make a thick paste. Whisk in a little more stock to make a smooth liquid.

3 Melt the butter in heavy-based saucepan over a medium-low heat. Add the onion, cover and cook for about 5 minutes, stirring frequently, until it softens.

4 Add the remaining fish stock and bring to the boil. Slowly whisk in the flour mixture until well combined and bring back to the boil, whisking constantly. Add the mussel cooking liquid. Season with salt, if needed, and pepper. Reduce the heat and simmer, partially covered, for 15 minutes.

5 Add the fish and mussels and continue simmering, stirring occasionally, for about 5 minutes, or until the fish is cooked and begins to flake.

6 Stir in the prawns and cream. Taste and adjust the seasoning. Simmer for a few minutes to heat through. Ladle into warm bowls, sprinkle with dill and serve.

Smoked Haddock Soup

This chunky, aromatic soup is perfect for a cold-weather lunch or supper served with crusty bread and a salad.

NUTRITIONAL INFORMATION

Calories 80   Sugars 2.9g
Protein . . . . .4.3g   Fat 3g
Carbohydrate . . .9.6g   Saturates 1.4g

5–10 mins   40 mins

SERVES 4

I N G R E D I E N T S

1 tbsp oil

55 g/2 oz smoked streaky bacon, cut into matchsticks

1 large onion, finely chopped

2 tbsp plain flour

1 litre/1¾ pints milk

700 g/1 lb 9 oz potatoes, cubed

175 g/6 oz skinless smoked haddock

salt and pepper

finely chopped fresh parsley, to garnish

1 Heat the oil in a large saucepan over a medium heat. Add the pieces of bacon and cook them for 2 minutes. Stir in the chopped onion and continue cooking for 5–7 minutes, stirring frequently, until the onion is soft and the bacon a golden colour. Now tip the pan and spoon off as much fat as possible.

2 Stir in the flour and continue cooking for 2 minutes. Add half of the milk and stir well, scraping the bottom of the pan to mix in the flour.

3 Add the potatoes and remaining milk and season with pepper. Bring just to the boil, stirring frequently, then reduce the heat and simmer, partially covered, for 10 minutes.

4 Add the fish and continue cooking, stirring occasionally, for about 15 minutes, or until the potatoes are tender and the fish breaks up easily.

5 Taste the soup and adjust the seasoning if necessary (salt may not be needed). Ladle into a warm tureen or soup bowls and sprinkle generously with chopped parsley.

COOK'S TIP

Cutting the potatoes into small cubes not only looks attractive – it also allows them to cook more quickly and evenly.

Salmon & Leek Soup

Salmon is a favourite with almost everyone. This delicately flavoured and pretty soup is perfect for entertaining.

NUTRITIONAL INFORMATION

Calories	338	Sugars	.........7g
Protein	........19g	Fat	.........22g
Carbohydrate	...17g	Saturates	.......8g

10–15 mins   40 mins

SERVES 4

INGREDIENTS

1 tbsp olive oil

1 large onion, finely chopped

3 large leeks, including green parts, thinly sliced

1 potato, finely diced

450 ml/16 fl oz fish stock

700 ml/1¼ pints water

1 bay leaf

300 g/10½ oz skinless salmon fillet, cut into 1-cm/½-inch cubes

5 tbsp double cream

salt and pepper

fresh lemon juice (optional)

snipped fresh chervil or parsley, to garnish

1 Heat the oil in a heavy-based saucepan over a medium heat. Add the onion and leeks and cook for about 3 minutes until they begin to soften.

2 Add the potato, stock, water and bay leaf with a large pinch of salt. Bring to the boil, reduce the heat, cover and cook gently for about 25 minutes until the vegetables are tender. Remove the bay leaf.

3 Allow the soup to cool slightly, then transfer about half of it to a blender or food processor and purée until smooth. (If using a food processor, strain off the cooking liquid and reserve. Purée half the soup solids with enough cooking liquid to moisten them, then combine with the remaining liquid.)

4 Return the puréed soup to the saucepan and stir to blend. Reheat gently over a medium-low heat.

5 Season the salmon with salt and pepper and add to the soup. Continue cooking for about 5 minutes, stirring occasionally, until the fish is tender and starts to break up. Stir in the cream, taste and adjust the seasoning, adding a little lemon juice if wished. Ladle into warm bowls, sprinkle with chervil or parsley and serve.

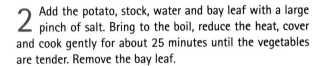
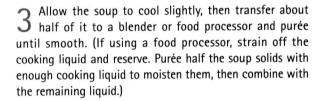
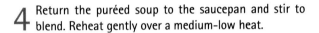

Breton Fish Soup with Cider

Fishermen's soups are variable, depending on the season and the catch. Monkfish has a texture like lobster, but tender cod is equally appealing.

NUTRITIONAL INFORMATION

Calories 103	Sugars 1.5g
Protein 5.2g	Fat 6.3g
Carbohydrate . . .6.6g	Saturates 3.8g

5–10 mins   40 mins

SERVES 4

INGREDIENTS

2 tsp butter

1 large leek, thinly sliced

2 shallots, finely chopped

300ml/10 fl oz cider

125 ml/4 fl oz fish stock

250 g/9 oz potatoes, diced

1 bay leaf

4 tbsp plain flour

175 ml/6 fl oz milk

175 ml/6 fl oz double cream

55 g/2 oz fresh sorrel leaves

350 g/12 oz skinless monkfish or cod fillet, cut into 2.5-cm/1-inch pieces

salt and pepper

COOK'S TIP

Be careful not to overcook the fish, otherwise tender fish, such as cod, breaks up into smaller and smaller flakes, and firm fish, such as monkfish, can become tough.

1 Melt the butter in a large saucepan over a medium-low heat. Add the leek and shallots and cook for about 5 minutes, stirring frequently, until they start to soften. Add the cider and bring to the boil.

2 Stir in the stock, potatoes and bay leaf with a large pinch of salt (unless the stock is salty) and bring back to the boil. Reduce the heat, cover the pan and cook the soup gently for 10 minutes.

3 Put the flour in a small bowl and very slowly whisk in a few tablespoons of the milk to make a thick paste. Stir in more milk, if needed, to make a smooth liquid.

4 Adjust the heat so that the soup bubbles gently. Stir in the flour mixture and cook, stirring frequently, for 5 minutes. Add the remaining milk and half the cream. Continue cooking for about 10 minutes until the potatoes are tender.

5 Chop the sorrel finely and combine with the remaining cream. (If using a food processor, add the sorrel and chop, then add the cream and process briefly.)

6 Stir the sorrel cream into the soup and add the fish. Continue cooking, stirring occasionally, for about 3 minutes, until the monkfish stiffens or the cod just begins to flake. Taste the soup and adjust the seasoning, if necessary. Ladle into warm bowls and serve.

Saffron Fish Soup

This elegant soup makes a good dinner party starter. To make planning easier, the saffron-flavoured soup base can be made ahead of time.

NUTRITIONAL INFORMATION

Calories 329   Sugars 8g
Protein . . . . .19g   Fat 18g
Carbohydrate . . .17g   Saturates 11g

 10–15 mins   40 mins

SERVES 4

I N G R E D I E N T S

2 tsp butter

1 onion, finely chopped

1 leek, thinly sliced

1 carrot, thinly sliced

4 tbsp white rice

pinch of saffron threads

125 ml/4 fl oz dry white wine

1 litre/1¾ pints fish stock

125 ml/4 fl oz double cream

350 g/12 oz skinless white fish fillet, such as cod, haddock or monkfish, cut into 1-cm/½-inch cubes

4 tomatoes, skinned, deseeded and chopped

3 tbsp snipped fresh chives, to garnish

salt and pepper

1 Heat the butter in a saucepan over a medium heat and add the onion, leek and carrot. Cook for 3–4 minutes, stirring frequently, until the onion is soft.

2 Add the rice, saffron, wine and stock, bring just to the boil and reduce the heat to low. Season with salt and pepper. Cover and simmer for 20 minutes, or until the rice and vegetables are soft.

3 Transfer the soup to a blender and purée until smooth. (If using a food processor, purée the solids with enough cooking liquid to moisten them, then combine with the remaining liquid.)

4 Return the soup to the saucepan, stir in the cream and simmer over a low heat for a few minutes until heated through, stirring occasionally.

5 Season the fish and add, together with the tomatoes, to the simmering soup. Cook for 3–5 minutes, or until the fish is just tender.

6 Stir in most of the chives. Taste the soup and adjust the seasoning, if necessary. Ladle the soup into warm shallow bowls, sprinkle the remaining chives on top and serve.

Curried Tuna Chowder

This tasty soup uses canned tuna and tomatoes, two storecupboard favourites that you are likely to have on hand, for a quickly made lunch.

NUTRITIONAL INFORMATION

Calories 239	Sugars 5g
Protein 16g	Fat 11g
Carbohydrate . . .20g	Saturates 7g

 5–10 mins   40–50 mins

SERVES 3–4

I N G R E D I E N T S

200 g/7 oz canned light meat tuna packed in water

1½ tbsp butter

1 onion, finely chopped

1 garlic clove, finely chopped

2 tbsp plain flour

2 tsp mild curry powder

400 g/14 oz canned plum tomatoes in juice

3 tbsp white rice

1 courgette, finely diced

125 ml/4 fl oz single cream

salt and pepper

1 Drain the tuna over a measuring jug and add boiling water to make up to 600 ml/1 pint.

2 Melt the butter in a large saucepan over a medium-low heat. Add the onion and garlic and cook for about 5 minutes until the onion is softened, stirring frequently.

3 Stir in the flour and curry powder. Continue cooking for 2 minutes.

4 Slowly add about half of the tuna juice and water mixture and stir well, scraping the bottom of the pan to mix in the flour. Pour in the remaining mixture and bring just to the boil, stirring frequently. Add the tomatoes and break up with a spoon. When the soup almost comes back to the boil, stir in the rice, reduce the heat, cover and simmer for about 10 minutes.

5 Add the tuna and courgette to the soup and continue cooking for about 15 minutes, or until the vegetables and rice are tender.

6 Stir in the cream, season with salt and pepper to taste and continue simmering for about 3–4 minutes until heated through. Ladle the soup into warm bowls and serve.

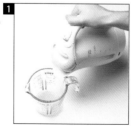

Potato & Mixed Fish Soup

Any mixture of fish is suitable for this recipe, from simple smoked and white fish to salmon or mussels, depending on the occasion.

NUTRITIONAL INFORMATION

Calories 458   Sugars 5g
Protein ....28g   Fat 25g
Carbohydrate ...22g   Saturates 12g

🍴 10 mins   🕐 35 mins

SERVES 4

INGREDIENTS

2 tbsp vegetable oil

450 g/1 lb small new potatoes, halved

1 bunch spring onions, sliced

1 yellow pepper, sliced

2 garlic cloves, crushed

225 ml/8 fl oz dry white wine

600 ml/1 pint fish stock

225 g/8 oz white fish fillet, skinned and cubed

225 g/8 oz smoked cod fillet, skinned and cubed

2 tomatoes, peeled, seeded and chopped

100 g/3½ oz peeled cooked prawns

150 ml/¼ pint double cream

2 tbsp shredded fresh basil

1 Heat the vegetable oil in a large saucepan and add the potatoes, sliced spring onions, pepper and garlic. Sauté gently for 3 minutes, stirring constantly.

2 Add the white wine and fish stock to the saucepan and bring to the boil. Reduce the heat and simmer the mixture for about 10–15 minutes.

3 Add the cubed fish fillets and the tomatoes to the soup and continue to cook for 10 minutes or until the fish is cooked through.

4 Stir in the prawns, cream and shredded basil and cook for 2–3 minutes. Pour the soup into warmed bowls and serve immediately.

COOK'S TIP
For a soup that is slightly less rich, omit the wine and stir natural yogurt into the soup instead of the double cream.

Mexican Fish Soup

Mexico's long shoreline yields an abundance of fish and shellfish, which are often turned into spicy, satisfying soups.

NUTRITIONAL INFORMATION

Calories	220	Sugars	.........6g
Protein	........27g	Fat	..........10g
Carbohydrate	....7g	Saturates	.......1g

 10–15 mins   50 mins

SERVES 4

INGREDIENTS

5 ripe tomatoes

5 garlic cloves, unpeeled

500 g/1 lb 2 oz snapper, cut into chunks

1 litre/1¾ pints fish stock or water, plus a fish stock cube or two

2–3 tbsp olive oil

1 onion, chopped

2 fresh chillies, such as serrano, deseeded and thinly sliced

lime wedges, to serve

1 Heat an ungreased heavy-based frying pan, add the whole tomatoes and garlic and char over a high heat or under a preheated grill. The skins of the vegetables should blacken and char, and the flesh inside should be tender. Alternatively, place the tomatoes and garlic cloves in a roasting tin and bake in a preheated oven at 190–200°C/ 375–400°F/ Gas Mark 5–6 for about 40 minutes.

2 Leave the tomatoes and garlic to cool, then remove the skins and chop roughly, combining them with any juices from the pan. Set aside.

3 Poach the snapper in the stock over medium heat until it is opaque and firmish. Remove from the heat, set aside.

4 Heat the oil in a pan and cook the onion until softened. Strain in the cooking liquid from the fish, then add the tomatoes and garlic, and stir.

5 Bring to the boil, then reduce the heat and simmer for about 5 minutes to combine the flavours. Add the chillies.

6 Divide chunks of the poached fish between soup bowls, ladle over the hot soup and serve with lime wedges for squeezing over the top.

Creamy Sweetcorn Soup

This speedy soup is a good storecupboard standby, made in a matter of minutes. If you prefer, you can use frozen crab sticks.

NUTRITIONAL INFORMATION

Calories 183	Sugars 9g
Protein 7g	Fat 6g
Carbohydrate . . .26g	Saturates 1g

5–10 mins   20 mins

SERVES 4

I N G R E D I E N T S

1 tbsp vegetable oil

3 garlic cloves, crushed

1 tsp fresh ginger root, grated

700 ml/1¼ pints chicken stock

375 g/13 oz canned creamed sweetcorn

1 tbsp Thai fish sauce

175 g/6 oz canned white crab meat, drained

1 egg

salt and pepper

fresh coriander, shredded, and paprika,
   to garnish

1 Heat the oil in a large saucepan and fry the garlic for about 1 minute, stirring constantly.

2 Add the ginger to the pan, then stir in the stock and creamed sweetcorn. Bring to the boil.

3 Stir in the fish sauce, crab meat and salt and pepper, then return the soup to the boil.

4 Beat the egg, then stir lightly into the soup so that it sets into long strands. Simmer gently for about 30 seconds.

5 Ladle the soup into bowls and serve hot, garnished with shredded coriander and sprinkled with paprika.

COOK'S TIP

To give the soup an extra-rich flavour kick for a special occasion, stir in 1 tablespoon of dry sherry or rice wine just before you ladle it into bowls.

Clam & Sorrel Soup

This recipe is intended to be served in small quantities, because the soup is very rich and full of flavour.

NUTRITIONAL INFORMATION

Calories 384	Sugars 4g	
Protein 18g	Fat 29g	
Carbohydrate 7g	Saturates 18g	

10–15 mins   30 mins

SERVES 4

INGREDIENTS

900 g/2 lb live clams, scrubbed

1 onion, finely chopped

150 ml/5 fl oz dry white wine

50 g/1¾ oz butter

1 small carrot, finely diced

2 shallots, finely diced

1 stick celery, finely diced

2 bay leaves

150 ml/5 fl oz double cream

25 g/1 oz loosely packed shredded sorrel

pepper

crusty bread, to serve

dill, to garnish

1 Put the clams into a large saucepan with the onion and wine. Cover and cook over a high heat for 3–4 minutes until the clams have opened. Strain, reserving the cooking liquid, but discarding the onion. Set aside the clams until they are cool enough to handle.

2 In a clean saucepan, melt the butter over a low heat. Add the carrot, shallots and celery and cook very gently for 10 minutes until softened but not coloured. Add the reserved cooking liquid and bay leaves and simmer the soup for a further 10 minutes.

3 Meanwhile, roughly chop the clams, if large. Add to the soup with the cream and sorrel. Simmer a further 2–3 minutes until the sorrel has collapsed. Season with pepper and serve immediately with plenty of crusty bread.

COOK'S TIP

Sorrel is a large-leafed herb with a slightly sour, lemony flavour that goes very well with fish. It is increasingly easy to find in larger supermarkets, but is also incredibly easy to grow, as a plant.

Thai Fishcakes

These little fishcakes are very popular in Thailand as street food, and make a perfect snack. Alternatively, serve them as a starter.

NUTRITIONAL INFORMATION

Calories	205	Sugars	.........6g
Protein	........17g	Fat	..........12g
Carbohydrate	....7g	Saturates	.......2g

 5–10 mins   30–40 mins

SERVES 4-5

INGREDIENTS

350 g/12 oz white fish fillet without skin, such as cod or haddock

1 tbsp Thai fish sauce

2 tsp Thai red curry paste

1 tbsp lime juice

1 garlic clove, crushed

4 dried kaffir lime leaves, crumbled

1 egg white

3 tbsp fresh coriander, chopped

salt and pepper

vegetable oil for shallow-frying

green salad leaves, to serve

PEANUT DIP

1 small red chilli

1 tbsp light soy sauce

1 tbsp lime juice

1 tbsp soft light brown sugar

3 tbsp chunky peanut butter

4 tbsp coconut milk

1 Put the fish fillet in a food processor along with the fish sauce, red curry paste, lime juice, garlic, lime leaves and egg white, and process the ingredients until a smooth paste forms.

2 Stir in the fresh coriander and quickly process the paste again until it is mixed. Divide the fish mixture into about 8–10 pieces and roll into balls, then flatten the balls to make round patties and set them aside.

3 For the dip, halve and deseed the chilli, then chop finely. Place in a small pan with the remaining dip ingredients and heat gently, stirring constantly, until well blended. Adjust the seasoning to taste.

4 Shallow-fry the fishcakes in batches for 3–4 minutes on each side until golden brown. Drain on kitchen paper and serve them hot on a bed of green salad leaves with the peanut dip.

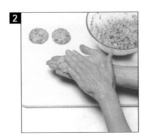

Bagna Cauda with Crudités

Translated literally, *bagna cauda* means 'hot bath'. This is a typical dish from Piedmont in Italy, where it is often eaten at large gatherings.

NUTRITIONAL INFORMATION

Calories 421	Sugars 6g
Protein 7g	Fat 33g
Carbohydrate . . .25g	Saturates 11g

 20–30 mins   5–10 mins

SERVES 8

INGREDIENTS

1 yellow pepper

3 sticks celery

2 carrots

½ cauliflower

115 g/4 oz mushrooms

1 bulb fennel

1 bunch spring onions

2 beetroot, cooked and peeled

8 radishes

225 g/8 oz boiled new potatoes

225 ml/8 fl oz olive oil (not extra-virgin)

5 garlic cloves, crushed

50 g/1¾ oz canned anchovies in oil, drained and chopped

115 g/4 oz butter

Italian bread, to serve

COOK'S TIP

If you have one, a fondue set is perfect for serving this dish as the sauce can be kept hot at the table.

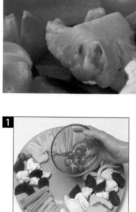

1 Prepare the vegetables. Deseed and slice the pepper thickly. Cut the celery into 7.5-cm/3-inch lengths. Cut the carrots into batons. Score the mushrooms as in the photograph. Separate the cauliflower into florets. Cut the fennel in half lengthways then cut each half into 4 lengthways. Trim the spring onions. Cut the beetroot into eighths. Trim the radishes. Cut the potatoes in half, if large. Arrange the prepared vegetables on a large serving platter.

2 Heat the oil very gently in a saucepan. Add the garlic and anchovies and cook very gently, stirring, until the anchovies have dissolved. Take care not to brown or burn the garlic.

3 Add the butter and as soon as it has melted, serve straight away with the selection of crudités and plenty of bread.

Smoked Mackerel Pâté

This is a quick and easy pâté with plenty of flavour. It originates from Goa, on the west coast of India, an area famous for its seafood.

25–30 mins, plus refrigeration time

5–10 mins

SERVES 4

INGREDIENTS

200 g/7 oz smoked mackerel fillet

1 small, hot green chilli, deseeded and chopped

1 garlic clove, chopped

3 tbsp fresh coriander leaves

150 ml/5 fl oz soured cream

1 small red onion, chopped

2 tbsp lime juice

salt and pepper

4 slices white bread, crusts removed

1. Skin and flake the mackerel fillet, removing any small bones. Put the flesh in the bowl of a food processor along with the chilli, garlic, coriander and soured cream. Blend until smooth.

2. Transfer the mixture to a bowl and mix in the onion and lime juice. Season to taste. The pâté will seem very soft at this stage but will firm up in the refrigerator. Refrigerate for several hours or overnight if possible.

3. The pâté is served with melba toast. To make it, place the trimmed bread slices under a preheated medium grill and toast lightly on both sides. Split each piece in half horizontally, then cut these across diagonally to form 4 triangles per slice.

4. Put the melba toast triangles, untoasted side up, under the grill and toast them until they are golden and curled at the edges. Serve the toast warm or cold with the pâté.

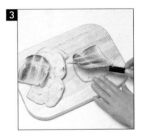

Gravadlax

You need two pieces of salmon fillet for this dish, approximately the same size. Ask your fishmonger to remove all the bones and scale the fish.

NUTRITIONAL INFORMATION

Calories	608	Sugars	........11g
Protein	........37g	Fat	..........34g
Carbohydrate	...41g	Saturates	......14g

30–40 mins, plus refrigeration time   0 mins

SERVES 6

INGREDIENTS

2 x 450 g/1 lb salmon fillets, with skin on

6 tbsp roughly chopped fresh dill

115 g/4 oz sea salt

50 g/1¾ oz sugar

1 tbsp white peppercorns, roughly crushed

12 slices brown bread, buttered, to serve

GARNISH

lemon slices

dill sprigs

1 Wash the salmon fillets and dry with kitchen paper. Put one fillet, skin side down, in a non-metallic dish.

2 Mix together the dill, sea salt, sugar and peppercorns. Spread this mixture over the first fillet of fish and place the second fillet, skin side up, on top. Put a plate, the same size as the fish, on top and put a weight on the plate (3 or 4 cans of tomatoes or similar will do).

3 Refrigerate for 2 days, turning the salmon fillets about every 12 hours and basting with any juices that have come out of the fish.

4 Remove the salmon from the brine and slice thinly, without slicing the skin, as you would smoked salmon. Cut the brown bread into triangles and serve with the salmon. Garnish with lemon wedges and sprigs of fresh dill.

COOK'S TIP

You can brush the marinade off the salmon before slicing, but the line of green along the edge of the salmon is quite attractive and, of course, full of flavour.

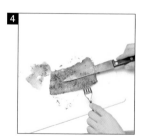

Thai-style Crab Sandwich

A hearty, open sandwich, topped with a classic flavour combination – crab with avocado and ginger. Perfect for a light summer lunch.

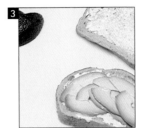

NUTRITIONAL INFORMATION

Calories	768	Sugars	..........3g
Protein	........26g	Fat	..........49g
Carbohydrate	...58g	Saturates	.......8g

40 mins

0 mins

SERVES 2

INGREDIENTS

2 tbsp lime juice

2 cm/¾ inch piece fresh ginger root, grated

2-cm/¾-inch piece lemon grass, finely chopped

5 tbsp mayonnaise

2 large slices crusty bread

1 ripe avocado

150 g/5½ oz cooked crab meat

black pepper, freshly ground

sprigs fresh coriander, to garnish

COOK'S TIP

To make mayonnaise flavoured with lime and ginger, place 2 egg yolks, 1 tablespoon lime juice and ½ teaspoon grated ginger root in a blender goblet. With the motor running, gradually add 300 ml/ 10 fl oz olive oil, drop by drop, until the mixture is thick and smooth. Season with salt and pepper.

1 Mix half the lime juice with the ginger and lemon grass. Add the mayonnaise and mix well.

2 Spread 1 tablespoon of mayonnaise smoothly over each slice of bread.

3 Halve the avocado and remove the stone. Peel and slice the flesh thinly, then arrange the slices on the bread. Sprinkle with lime juice.

4 Spoon the crab meat over the avocado, then add any remaining lime juice. Spoon over the remaining mayonnaise, season with freshly ground black pepper, top with a coriander sprig and serve immediately.

Steamed Yellow Fish Fillets

Thailand has an abundance of fresh fish, which is an important part of the local diet. Dishes such as these steamed fillets are popular.

NUTRITIONAL INFORMATION

Calories	165	Sugars	.........1g
Protein	........23g	Fat	...........2g
Carbohydrate	...13g	Saturates	.......1g

40 mins   15 mins

SERVES 3-4

I N G R E D I E N T S

500 g/1 lb 2 oz firm fish fillets, such as red snapper, sole or monkfish

1 dried red bird's-eye chilli

1 small onion, chopped

3 garlic cloves, chopped

2 sprigs fresh coriander

1 tsp coriander seeds

½ tsp turmeric

½ tsp ground black pepper

1 tbsp Thai fish sauce

2 tbsp coconut milk

1 small egg, beaten

2 tbsp rice flour

red and green chilli strips, to garnish

soy sauce, to serve

1 Remove any skin from the fish and cut the fillets diagonally into long 2-cm/¾-inch wide strips.

2 Place the dried chilli, onion, garlic, coriander and coriander seeds in a pestle and mortar and grind until they are a smooth paste.

3 Add the turmeric, pepper, fish sauce, coconut milk and beaten egg, stirring well to mix evenly.

4 Dip the fish strips into the paste mixture, then into the rice flour to coat lightly.

5 Bring the water in a steamer to the boil, then arrange the fish strips in the top of the steamer. Cover and steam for about 12–15 minutes until the fish is just firm.

6 Serve the fish with soy sauce and an accompaniment of stir-fried vegetables or salad.

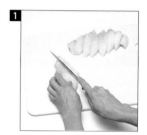

COOK'S TIP

If you don't have a steamer, improvise by placing a large metal colander over a large pan of boiling water and cover with an upturned plate to enclose the fish as it steams.

Sesame & Coriander Noodles

Delicately scented with sesame and coriander, these noodles make an unusual lunch or supper dish.

NUTRITIONAL INFORMATION

Calories	430	Sugars	.........2g
Protein	........23g	Fat	..........15g
Carbohydrate	...56g	Saturates	.......3g

20–30 mins   15 mins

SERVES 4

I N G R E D I E N T S

1 garlic clove, chopped

1 spring onion, chopped

1 small red chilli, deseeded and sliced

1 handful fresh coriander

300 g/10½ oz fine egg noodles

2 tbsp vegetable oil

2 tsp sesame oil

1 tsp shrimp paste

225 g/8 oz raw prawns, peeled

2 tbsp lime juice

2 tbsp Thai fish sauce

1 tsp sesame seeds, toasted

COOK'S TIP

The roots of coriander are widely used in Thai cooking, so if you can buy fresh coriander with the root attached, the whole plant can be used in this dish for maximum flavour. If not, just use the stems and leaves.

1 Place the garlic, spring onion, chilli and coriander in a pestle and mortar and grind to a smooth paste.

2 Drop the noodles into a pan of boiling water. Simmer for 4 minutes, or according to the package directions.

3 Meanwhile, heat the oils in a wok and stir in the shrimp paste and ground coriander mixture. Stir over a medium heat for 1 minute.

4 Stir in the prawns and stir-fry for 2 minutes. Stir in the lime juice and fish sauce and cook for a further minute.

5 Drain the noodles and toss them into the wok. Sprinkle with the sesame seeds and serve.

Hot-smoked Salmon Scramble

Unlike traditional smoked salmon, the fish is smoked in a hot environment so that the flesh cooks conventionally but has a wonderful smoky flavour.

NUTRITIONAL INFORMATION

Calories	679	Sugars	.........3g
Protein	........37g	Fat	..........45g
Carbohydrate	...35g	Saturates	......20g

10–15 mins   30 mins

SERVES 4

INGREDIENTS

4 tbsp butter

8 eggs, lightly beaten

4 tbsp double cream

225 g/8 oz skinless, boneless, hot-smoked salmon, flaked

2 tbsp chopped fresh mixed herbs such as chives, basil, parsley

4 English muffins, split

extra butter, for spreading

salt and pepper

chopped fresh chives, to garnish

lemon wedges, to serve

VARIATION

If you have difficulty finding hot-smoked salmon, you could substitute conventional smoked salmon, chopped.

1 Melt the butter in a large frying pan and when it begins to foam, add the eggs. Leave for a moment until the eggs start to set and then slowly stir and move the set eggs away from the bottom of the frying pan to allow uncooked egg to take its place. Leave again for a moment and repeat the process.

2 Before all the egg has set, stir in the double cream, flaked salmon and chopped herbs. Stir to incorporate. Take care not to overcook the eggs.

3 Meanwhile, toast the muffins on both sides. Spread with more butter if liked. Place 2 halves on each of 4 plates.

4 When the eggs are cooked, divide between the muffins. Sprinkle over a few chopped chives, season and serve while still warm with a lemon wedge.

Cullen Skink

This is a traditional, creamy Scottish soup. As the smoked haddock has quite a strong flavour, it has been mixed with some fresh cod.

NUTRITIONAL INFORMATION

Calories 108   Sugars 2.3g
Protein . . . . .7.4g   Fat 6.4g
Carbohydrate . . .5.6g   Saturates 3.9g

 20 mins   40 mins

SERVES 4

I N G R E D I E N T S

225 g/8 oz undyed smoked haddock fillet

2 tbsp butter

1 onion, finely chopped

600 ml/1 pint milk

350 g/12 oz potatoes, diced

350 g/12 oz cod, boned, skinned and cubed

150 ml/5 fl oz double cream

2 tbsp chopped fresh parsley

lemon juice, to taste

salt and pepper

T O   G A R N I S H

lemon slices

parsley sprigs

1 Put the haddock fillet in a large frying pan and cover with boiling water. Leave for 10 minutes. Drain, reserving 300 ml/10 fl oz of the soaking water. Flake the fish and remove all the bones.

2 Heat the butter in a large saucepan and add the onion. Cook gently for 10 minutes until softened. Add the milk and bring to a gentle simmer before adding the potatoes. Cook for 10 minutes.

3 Add the reserved haddock flakes and cod. Simmer for an additional 10 minutes until the cod is tender.

4 Remove about one-third of the fish and potatoes, put in a food processor and blend until smooth. Alternatively, push the mixture through a sieve into a bowl. Return to the soup with the cream, parsley and seasoning. Taste and add a little lemon juice, if desired. Add a little of the reserved soaking water if the soup seems too thick. Reheat gently and serve the soup immediately, garnished with parsley and lemon slices.

COOK'S TIP
Look for Finnan haddock, if you can find it. Do not use yellow-dyed haddock fillet, which is often whiting and actually not haddock at all.

Basque Tuna Stew

Although versions of this stew are eaten throughout Spain, it originated in the Basque region.

NUTRITIONAL INFORMATION

Calories	110	Sugars	.........8g
Protein	........10g	Fat	...........2g
Carbohydrate	...13g	Saturates	.......0g

10–15 mins   40 mins

SERVES 4

I N G R E D I E N T S

5 tbsp olive oil

1 large onion, chopped

2 garlic cloves, chopped

200 g/7 oz canned chopped tomatoes

700 g/1 lb 9 oz potatoes, cut into 5-cm/2-inch chunks

3 green peppers, deseeded and roughly chopped

300 ml/10 fl oz cold water

900 g/2 lb fresh tuna, cut into chunks

4 slices crusty white bread

salt and pepper

VARIATION

Substitute any very firm-fleshed fish, such as shark or swordfish, for the tuna used in this recipe.

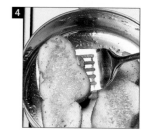

1 Heat 2 tablespoons of the oil in a saucepan and add the onion. Cook for 8–10 minutes until soft and brown. Add the garlic and cook a further minute. Add the tomatoes, cover and simmer for 30 minutes until thickened.

2 Meanwhile, in a clean saucepan, mix together the potatoes and peppers. Add the water (which should just cover the vegetables). Bring to the boil and simmer for 15 minutes until the potatoes are almost cooked through.

3 Add the tuna and the tomato mixture to the potatoes and peppers and season. Cover and simmer for 6–8 minutes until the tuna is tender.

4 Meanwhile, heat the remaining oil in a large frying pan over a medium heat and add the bread slices. Fry them on both sides until golden. Drain on kitchen paper. Serve with the stew.

Barbecued Monkfish

Monkfish cooks very well on a barbecue because it is a firm-fleshed fish. The marinade adds a tang of lime and ginger.

NUTRITIONAL INFORMATION

Calories 219   Sugars 0.1g
Protein . . . . .28g   Fat 12g
Carbohydrate . . . .1g   Saturates 2g

 30–40 mins, plus marinating time   5–6 mins

SERVES 4

I N G R E D I E N T S

4 tbsp olive oil

grated rind of 1 lime

2 tsp Thai fish sauce

2 garlic cloves, crushed

1 tsp grated fresh ginger root

2 tbsp chopped fresh basil

700 g/1 lb 9 oz monkfish fillet, cut into chunks

2 limes, each cut into 6 wedges

salt and pepper

1 Mix together the olive oil, lime rind, fish sauce, garlic, ginger and basil. Season and set aside.

2 Wash and dry the chunks of fish. Add them to the marinade and mix well. Leave to marinate for 2 hours, stirring occasionally.

3 If you are using bamboo skewers, soak them in cold water for 30 minutes. Then, lift the monkfish pieces from the marinade and thread them on to the skewers, alternating with the lime wedges.

4 Transfer the skewers to a lit barbecue or a preheated ridged grill pan. Cook for 5–6 minutes, turning regularly, until the fish is tender. Serve immediately.

VARIATION

You could use any type of white-fleshed fish for this recipe but sprinkle the pieces with salt and leave for 2 hours to firm the flesh, before rinsing, drying and then adding to the marinade.

Swordfish or Tuna Fajitas

Fajitas are usually made with chicken or lamb but using a firm fish like swordfish or tuna works very well.

NUTRITIONAL INFORMATION

Calories	766	Sugars	........12g
Protein	........52g	Fat	..........36g
Carbohydrate	...63g	Saturates	......10g

30 mins, plus marinating time

20 mins

SERVES 4

INGREDIENTS

3 tbsp olive oil

2 tsp chilli powder

1 tsp ground cumin

pinch cayenne pepper

1 garlic clove, crushed

900 g/2 lb swordfish or tuna

1 red pepper, deseeded and thinly sliced

1 yellow pepper, deseeded and thinly sliced

2 courgettes, cut into batons

1 large onion, thinly sliced

12 soft flour tortillas

1 tbsp lemon juice

3 tbsp chopped fresh coriander

salt and pepper

150 ml/5 fl oz soured cream, to serve

GUACAMOLE

1 large avocado

1 tomato, skinned, deseeded and diced

1 garlic clove, crushed

dash Tabasco

2 tbsp lemon juice

salt and pepper

1 Mix together the oil, chilli powder, cumin, cayenne and garlic. Cut the fish into chunks and mix with the marinade. Set aside for 1–2 hours.

2 Heat a large frying pan until hot. Put in the fish and its marinade and cook for 2 minutes, stirring occasionally, until the fish begins to brown. Add the peppers, courgettes and onion and cook for 5 minutes until the vegetables have softened but are still firm.

3 Meanwhile, warm the tortillas in a low oven or microwave.

4 To make the guacamole, mash the avocado and stir in the tomato, garlic, Tabasco, lemon juice and seasoning.

5 Add the lemon juice, coriander and seasoning to the vegetable mix. Spoon some of the mixture on the warmed tortilla. Top with guacamole and a spoonful of soured cream and roll up.

Tuna Fishcakes

These fishcakes make a satisfying supper. The tomato sauce has a tempting combination of lemon, garlic and basil.

NUTRITIONAL INFORMATION

Calories 638	Sugars 5g
Protein 35g	Fat 40g
Carbohydrate . . .38g	Saturates 5g

 5 mins   1 hr 10 mins

SERVES 4

INGREDIENTS

225 g/8 oz potatoes, cubed

1 tbsp olive oil

1 large shallot, finely chopped

1 garlic clove, finely chopped

1 tsp thyme leaves

400 g/14 oz canned tuna in olive oil, drained

grated rind ½ lemon

1 tbsp chopped fresh parsley

2–3 tbsp plain flour

1 egg, lightly beaten

115 g/4 oz fresh breadcrumbs

vegetable oil, for shallow-frying

salt and pepper

QUICK TOMATO SAUCE

2 tbsp olive oil

400 g/14 oz canned chopped tomatoes

1 garlic clove, crushed

½ tsp sugar

grated rind ½ lemon

1 tbsp chopped fresh basil

salt and pepper

1 For the tuna fishcakes, cook the potatoes in plenty of salted boiling water for 12–15 minutes until tender. Mash, leaving a few lumps, and set aside.

2 Heat the oil in a small frying pan and cook the shallot gently for 5 minutes until softened. Add the garlic and thyme leaves and cook for a further minute. Allow to cool slightly and then add to the potatoes with the tuna, lemon rind, parsley and seasoning. Mix together well but leave some texture.

3 Form the mixture into 6–8 cakes. Dip the cakes first in flour, then the egg and finally the breadcrumbs to coat. Refrigerate for 30 minutes.

4 Meanwhile, make the tomato sauce. Put the olive oil, tomatoes, garlic, sugar, lemon rind, basil and seasoning into a saucepan and bring to the boil. Cover and simmer gently for 30 minutes. Uncover and simmer for 15 minutes until thickened.

5 Heat enough oil to generously cover the bottom of a frying pan. When hot, add the fishcakes in batches and fry for 3-4 minutes each side until golden and crisp. Drain on kitchen paper. Serve hot with the tomato sauce.

Sardines with Pesto

This is a very quick and tasty midweek supper dish. Use a good-quality ready-made pesto for an even speedier meal.

NUTRITIONAL INFORMATION

Calories 617	Sugars 0.1g
Protein 27g	Fat 56g
Carbohydrates 1g	Saturates 11g

 30 mins   10 mins

SERVES 4

I N G R E D I E N T S

16 large sardines, scaled and gutted

50 g/1¾ oz fresh basil leaves

2 garlic cloves, crushed

2 tbsp pine kernels, toasted

50 g/1¾ oz freshly grated Parmesan cheese

150 ml/5 fl oz olive oil

salt and pepper

lemon wedges, to serve

1 Wash and dry the sardines and arrange on a grill pan.

2 Put the basil leaves, garlic and pine kernels in a food processor. Blend until finely chopped. Scrape the mixture out of the food processor, put in a bowl and stir in the Parmesan cheese and olive oil. Season to taste.

3 Spread a little of the pesto sauce over one side of the sardines and place under a preheated hot grill for 3 minutes. Turn the fish, spread with more pesto, and grill for a further 3 minutes until the sardines are cooked.

4 Serve immediately with extra pesto and lemon wedges.

VARIATION

This treatment will also work well with other small oily fish such as herrings and pilchards.

Salmon Frittata

A frittata is an Italian slow-cooked omelette, similar to the Spanish tortilla. Here it is filled with poached salmon.

NUTRITIONAL INFORMATION

Calories	300	Sugars	.........5g
Protein	........22g	Fat	..........21g
Carbohydrate	....7g	Saturates	.......8g

15 mins   40 mins

SERVES 6

INGREDIENTS

250 g/9 oz skinless, boneless salmon

3 sprigs fresh thyme

fresh parsley: 1 sprig, 2 tbsp chopped

5 black peppercorns

½ small onion, sliced

½ stick celery, sliced

½ carrot, chopped

175 g/6 oz asparagus spears, chopped

85 g/3 oz baby carrots, halved

4 tbsp butter

1 large onion, finely sliced

1 garlic clove, finely chopped

115 g/4 oz peas, fresh or frozen

8 eggs, lightly beaten

1 tbsp chopped fresh dill

salt and pepper

lemon wedges, to garnish

TO SERVE

crème fraîche, salad and crusty bread

1 Place the salmon in a saucepan with 1 sprig each of thyme and parsley, peppercorns, onion, celery and carrot. Cover with cold water and bring slowly to the boil. Remove from the heat and leave to stand for 5 minutes. Lift the fish out, flake the flesh and set aside.

2 Bring a large saucepan of salted water to the boil and blanch the asparagus for 2 minutes. Drain and refresh under cold water. Blanch the baby carrots for 4 minutes. Drain again and pat dry. Set aside.

3 Heat half the butter in a large frying pan and add the onion. Cook gently for 8–10 minutes until softened but not coloured. Add the chopped garlic and the remaining sprigs of thyme and cook for a further minute. Add the asparagus, carrots and peas and heat through. Remove from the heat.

4 Add the vegetables to the eggs with the chopped parsley, dill, salmon and seasoning and stir briefly. Heat the remaining butter in the pan and add the mixture. Cover and cook over a low heat for 10 minutes.

5 Cook under a preheated grill for a further 5 minutes until set and golden. Serve hot or cold in wedges topped with a dollop of crème fraîche, salad and crusty bread. Garnish with lemon wedges.

Mixed Seafood Brochettes

If your fishmonger sells turbot steaks, you will need one large steak for this dish. Remove the skin and bones and chop the flesh into chunks.

NUTRITIONAL INFORMATION

Calories 455	Sugars 0.1g	
Protein 32g	Fat 20g	
Carbohydrate ...39g	Saturates 9g	

🖐 🖐 🖐

🍲 30 mins, plus marinating time   🕐 20 mins

SERVES 4

I N G R E D I E N T S

225 g/8 oz skinless, boneless turbot fillet

225 g/8 oz skinless, boneless salmon fillet

8 scallops

8 large tiger prawns or langoustines

16 fresh bay leaves

1 lemon, sliced

4 tbsp olive oil

grated rind 1 lemon

4 tbsp chopped mixed herbs such as thyme, parsley, chives, basil

black pepper

L E M O N   B U T T E R   R I C E

175 g/6 oz long-grain rice

grated rind and juice 1 lemon

4 tbsp butter

salt and pepper

T O   G A R N I S H

lemon wedges

dill sprigs

1 Chop the turbot and salmon into 8 pieces each. Thread on to 8 skewers, with the scallops and tiger prawns or langoustines, alternating with the bay leaves and lemon slices. Put the brochettes into a non-metallic dish in a single layer if possible.

2 Mix together the oil, lemon rind, herbs and black pepper. Pour over the fish. Cover and leave to marinate for 2 hours, turning once or twice.

3 To make the lemon butter rice, bring a large saucepan of salted water to the boil and add the rice and grated lemon rind. Return to the boil and simmer for about 7–8 minutes until the rice is tender. Drain well and immediately stir the lemon juice and butter into the rice and lemon. Season with salt and pepper to taste.

4 Meanwhile, lift the fish brochettes from their marinade and cook on a lit barbecue or in a ridged grill pan under a preheated hot grill for 8–10 minutes, turning regularly, until cooked through. Serve with lemon butter rice. Garnish with lemon wedges and dill.

Chargrilled Scallops

Marinated scallops, chargrilled and served with couscous studded with colourful vegetables and herbs.

NUTRITIONAL INFORMATION

Calories	401	Sugars	.........3g
Protein	........20g	Fat	..........21g
Carbohydrate	...34g	Saturates	.......3g

10 mins, plus marinating time

35 mins

SERVES 4

I N G R E D I E N T S

16 king scallops

3 tbsp olive oil

grated rind 1 lime

2 tbsp chopped fresh basil

2 tbsp chopped fresh chives

1 garlic clove, finely chopped

black pepper

J E W E L L E D   C O U S C O U S

225 g/ 8 oz couscous

½ yellow pepper, deseeded and halved

½ red pepper, deseeded and halved

4 tbsp extra-virgin olive oil

115 g/4 oz cucumber, chopped into 1-cm/½-inch pieces

3 spring onions, finely chopped

1 tbsp lime juice

2 tbsp shredded fresh basil

salt and pepper

T O   G A R N I S H

basil leaves

lime wedges

1 Clean and trim the scallops as necessary. Put into a non-metallic dish. Mix together the olive oil, lime rind, basil, chives, garlic and black pepper. Pour over the scallops and cover. Leave to marinate for 2 hours.

2 Cook the couscous according to the packet instructions, omitting any butter recommended. Brush the red and yellow pepper halves with a little of the olive oil and place under a preheated hot grill for 5–6 minutes, turning once, until the skins are blackened and the flesh is tender. Put the peppers into a plastic bag and leave until cool enough to handle. When cool, peel off the skins and chop the flesh into 1-cm/½-inch pieces. Add the peppers to the couscous with the remaining olive oil, cucumber, spring onions, lemon juice and seasoning. Set aside.

3 Lift the scallops from the marinade and thread on to 4 skewers. Cook on a lit barbecue or preheated ridged grill pan for 1 minute on each side, until charred and firm but not quite cooked through. Remove from the heat and allow to rest for 2 minutes.

4 Stir the shredded basil into the couscous and divide on to plates. Put a skewer on each, garnish with basil leaves and lime wedges.

Prawn Rostis

These crisp little vegetable and prawn cakes make an ideal light lunch or supper, accompanied by a salad.

NUTRITIONAL INFORMATION

Calories 445	Sugars 9g	
Protein 19g	Fat 29g	
Carbohydrate . . .29g	Saturates 4g	

🥔 10 mins   🕐 1 hr

SERVES 4

INGREDIENTS

350 g/12 oz potatoes

350 g/12 oz celeriac

1 carrot

½ small onion

225 g/8 oz cooked peeled prawns,
    thawed if frozen and well drained on
    kitchen paper

2½ tbsp plain flour

1 egg, lightly beaten

vegetable oil, for frying

salt and pepper

CHERRY TOMATO SALSA

225 g/8 oz mixed cherry tomatoes such
    as baby plum, yellow, orange
    or pear, quartered

½ small mango, finely diced

1 red chilli, deseeded and finely chopped

½ small red onion, finely chopped

1 tbsp chopped fresh coriander

1 tbsp chopped fresh chives

2 tbsp olive oil

2 tsp lemon juice

salt and pepper

1 For the salsa, mix the tomatoes, mango, chilli, onion, coriander, chives, olive oil, lemon juice and seasoning. Set aside for the flavours to infuse.

2 Using a food processor or the fine blade of a box grater, finely grate the potatoes, celeriac, carrot and onion. Mix together with the prawns, flour and egg. Season well and set aside.

3 Divide the prawn mixture into eight equal pieces. Press each piece into a greased 10-cm/4-inch cutter (if you only have one cutter, you can simply shape the rostis individually).

4 In a large frying pan, heat a shallow layer of oil. When hot, transfer the vegetable cakes, still in the cutters, to the frying pan, in four batches if necessary. When the oil sizzles underneath, remove the cutter. Fry gently, pressing down with a spatula, for 6–8 minutes on each side, until crisp and browned and the vegetables are tender. Drain on kitchen paper and keep warm in a preheated oven. Serve hot with the tomato salsa.

Tagliatelle with Broccoli

This is based on a Sicilian dish combining broccoli and anchovies, but lemon and garlic have been added for more flavour.

NUTRITIONAL INFORMATION

Calories	529	Sugars	.........4g
Protein	........17g	Fat	..........20g
Carbohydrate	...75g	Saturates	.......3g

15–20 mins   30 mins

SERVES 4

INGREDIENTS

6 tbsp olive oil

50 g/1¾ oz fresh white breadcrumbs

450g/1 lb broccoli, cut into small florets

350 g/12 oz dried tagliatelle

4 anchovy fillets, drained and chopped

2 garlic cloves, sliced

grated rind 1 lemon

large pinch chilli flakes

salt and pepper

freshly grated Parmesan cheese, to serve

1 Heat 2 tablespoons of the olive oil in a frying pan and add the breadcrumbs. Stir-fry over a medium heat for 4–5 minutes until golden and crisp. Drain on kitchen paper.

2 Bring a large pan of salted water to the boil and add the broccoli. Blanch for 3 minutes then drain, reserving the water. Refresh the broccoli under cold water and drain again. Pat dry on kitchen paper and set aside.

3 Bring the water back to the boil and add the tagliatelle. Cook according to the packet instructions until tender but still firm to the bite.

4 Meanwhile, pour out another 2 tablespoons of the olive oil into a large frying pan or wok, heat it and then add the anchovy fillets. Cook for a minute then mash the anchovies with a wooden spoon to a paste. Add the garlic, lemon rind and chilli flakes and cook gently for 2 minutes. Add the broccoli and cook for a further 3–4 minutes until hot.

5 Drain the cooked pasta and add the broccoli mixture with the remaining 2 tablespoons of the olive oil and seasoning. Toss together well.

6 Divide the tagliatelle between serving plates. Top with the fried breadcrumbs and grated Parmesan cheese, and serve the dish immediately.

Pasta Puttanesca

The story goes that this was a sauce made and eaten by Italian prostitutes who needed a quick and simple meal to keep them going.

NUTRITIONAL INFORMATION

Calories	359	Sugars	........10g
Protein	........10g	Fat	.........14g
Carbohydrate	...51g	Saturates	.......2g

15–20 mins   30 mins

SERVES 4

INGREDIENTS

3 tbsp extra-virgin olive oil

1 large red onion, finely chopped

4 anchovy fillets, drained

pinch chilli flakes

2 garlic cloves, finely chopped

400 g/14 oz canned chopped tomatoes

2 tbsp tomato purée

225 g/8 oz dried spaghetti

25 g/1 oz pitted black olives, roughly chopped

25 g/1 oz pitted green olives, roughly chopped

1 tbsp capers, drained and rinsed

4 sun-dried tomatoes, roughly chopped

salt and pepper

1 Heat the oil in a saucepan and add the onion, anchovies and chilli flakes. Cook for 10 minutes until softened and starting to brown. Add the garlic and cook for 30 seconds.

2 Add the tomatoes and tomato purée and bring to the boil. Simmer gently for 10 minutes.

3 Meanwhile, cook the spaghetti in plenty of salted boiling water, according to the packet instructions, until it is tender but still firm to the bite.

4 Add the olives, capers and sun-dried tomatoes to the sauce. Simmer for a further 2–3 minutes. Season to taste with salt and pepper.

5 Drain the pasta thoroughly and pour in the anchovy sauce. Toss together so the pasta is well coated with sauce. Serve immediately.

Seafood Lasagne

A rich dish of layers of pasta, with seafood and mushrooms in a tomato sauce, topped with béchamel sauce and baked until golden.

NUTRITIONAL INFORMATION

Calories	790	Sugars	.......23g
Protein	........55g	Fat	..........32g
Carbohydrate	...74g	Saturates	......19g

30 mins   1 hr 20 mins

SERVES 6

INGREDIENTS

4 tbsp butter

6 tbsp flour

1 tsp mustard powder

600 ml/1 pint milk

2 tbsp olive oil

1 onion, chopped

2 garlic cloves, finely chopped

1 tbsp fresh thyme leaves

450 g/1 lb mixed mushrooms, sliced

150 ml/5 fl oz white wine

400 g/14 oz canned chopped tomatoes

450 g/1 lb mixed skinless white fish
  fillets, cubed

225 g/8 oz fresh scallops, trimmed

4–6 sheets fresh lasagne

225 g/8 oz mozzarella cheese, drained
  and chopped

salt and pepper

1 Melt the butter in a saucepan. Add the flour and mustard powder and stir until smooth. Simmer gently for 2 minutes without colouring. Gradually add the milk, whisking until smooth. Bring to the boil and simmer for 2 minutes. Remove from the heat and set aside. Cover the surface of the sauce with cling film to prevent a skin from forming.

2 Heat the oil in a frying pan and add the onion, garlic and thyme. Cook gently for 5 minutes until softened. Add the mushrooms and fry for a further 5 minutes until softened. Stir in the wine and boil rapidly until nearly evaporated. Stir in the tomatoes. Bring to the boil and simmer, covered, for 15 minutes. Season and set aside.

3 Grease a lasagne dish. Spoon half the tomato sauce in the dish and top with half the fish and scallops.

4 Layer half the lasagne over the fish, pour over half the white sauce, and add half the cubes of mozzarella. Repeat these layers, finishing with the white sauce and mozzarella.

5 Bake the lasagne in a preheated oven at 200°C/400°F/Gas Mark 6 for 35–40 minutes until bubbling and golden and the fish is cooked through. Remove from the oven and leave to stand on a heat-resistant surface or mat for 10 minutes before serving.

Spaghettini with Crab

This dish is probably one of the simplest in the book, yet the flavour is as impressive as that of a recipe over which you have slaved for hours.

NUTRITIONAL INFORMATION

Calories	488	Sugars	........3g
Protein	........13g	Fat	..........19g
Carbohydrate	...65g	Saturates	......3g

15–20 mins   20 mins

SERVES 4

I N G R E D I E N T S

1 dressed crab, about 450 g/1 lb including the shell

350 g/12 oz dried spaghettini

6 tbsp best-quality extra-virgin olive oil

1 hot red chilli, deseeded and finely chopped

2 garlic cloves, finely chopped

3 tbsp chopped fresh parsley

1 tsp finely grated lemon juice

2 tbsp lemon juice

salt and pepper

lemon wedges, to garnish

COOK'S TIP

If you prefer to buy your own fresh crab you will need a large crab weighing about 1 kg/2 lb 4 oz.

1 Scoop the meat from the crab shell and put it into into a bowl. Lightly mix the white and brown crab meat together and set aside.

2 Bring a large saucepan of salted water to the boil and add the spaghettini. Cook the pasta according to the instructions on the packet until it is tender but still firm to the bite. Drain well and return the spaghettini to the saucepan.

3 Meanwhile, heat 2 tablespoons of the olive oil in a frying pan. When hot, add the chilli and garlic. Cook for 30 seconds before adding the crab meat, parsley, lemon juice and lemon rind. Stir-fry for a further minute until the crab is just heated through.

4 Add the crab mixture to the pasta with the remaining olive oil and seasoning. Toss and serve immediately, garnished with lemon wedges.

Thai Noodles

The classic Thai noodle dish is flavoured with fish sauce, roasted peanuts and tiger prawns.

NUTRITIONAL INFORMATION

Calories ....344 Sugars 2g
Protein ....21g Fat 17g
Carbohydrate ...27g Saturates 2g

15 mins   30 mins

SERVES 4

INGREDIENTS

350 g/12 oz cooked, peeled tiger prawns

115 g/4 oz flat rice noodles or
  rice vermicelli

4 tbsp vegetable oil

2 garlic cloves, finely chopped

1 egg

2 tbsp lemon juice

1½ tbsp Thai fish sauce

½ tsp sugar

2 tbsp chopped, roasted peanuts

½ tsp cayenne pepper

2 spring onions, cut into
  2.5-cm/1-inch pieces

50 g/1¾ oz fresh beansprouts

1 tbsp chopped fresh coriander

lemon wedges, to serve

VARIATION

This is a basic dish to which lots of different cooked seafood could be added. Cooked squid rings, mussels and langoustines would all work just as well.

1 Drain the prawns on kitchen paper to remove excess moisture. Set aside. Cook the rice noodles or rice vermicelli according to the packet instructions. Drain well and set aside.

2 Heat the oil in a wok or large frying pan and add the garlic. Fry until just golden. Add the egg and stir quickly to break it up. Cook for a few seconds.

3 Add the prawns and noodles, scraping down the sides of the pan to ensure they mix with the egg and garlic.

4 Add the lemon juice, fish sauce, sugar, half the peanuts, cayenne pepper, spring onions and half the bean sprouts stirring quickly all the time. Cook over a high heat for a further 2 minutes until everything is heated through.

5 Turn on to a serving plate. Top with the remaining peanuts and beansprouts, and sprinkle with the coriander. Serve with lemon wedges.

Kedgeree

Originally, kedgeree or *khichri* was a Hindu dish of rice and lentils, varied with fish or meat in all kinds of ways.

NUTRITIONAL INFORMATION

Calories 457	Sugars 3g
Protein 33g	Fat 18g
Carbohydrate . . .40g	Saturates 6g

10–15 mins   30 mins

SERVES 4

INGREDIENTS

450 g/1 lb undyed smoked haddock fillet

2 tbsp olive oil

1 large onion, chopped

2 garlic cloves, finely chopped

½ tsp ground turmeric

½ tsp ground cumin

1 tsp ground coriander

175 g/6 oz basmati rice

4 medium eggs

2 tbsp butter

1 tbsp chopped fresh parsley

TO SERVE

lemon wedges

mango chutney

1 Pour boiling water over the haddock fillet and leave for 10 minutes. Lift the fish from the cooking water, discard the skin and bones and flake the fish. Set aside. Reserve the cooking water.

2 Heat the oil in a large saucepan and add the onion. Cook for 10 minutes over a medium heat until starting to brown. Add the garlic and cook for a further 30 seconds. Add the turmeric, cumin and coriander and stir-fry for 30 seconds until the spices smell fragrant. Add the rice and stir well.

3 Measure 350 ml/12 fl oz of the haddock cooking water and add this to the saucepan. Stir well and bring to the boil. Cover and cook over a very low heat for 12–15 minutes until the rice is tender and the stock is absorbed.

4 Meanwhile, bring a small saucepan of water to the boil and add the eggs. When the water has returned to the boil, cook the eggs for 8 minutes. Immediately drain the eggs and refresh them under cold water to stop them from cooking. Set them aside.

5 Add the reserved pieces of haddock, the butter and fresh parsley to the rice. Turn the rice on to a large serving dish. Shell and quarter the hard-boiled eggs and arrange them on top of the rice. Serve the kedgeree with lemon wedges and mango chutney.

A Modern Kedgeree

This is a modern version of the classic dish, using smoked salmon as well as fresh salmon and lots of fresh herbs.

NUTRITIONAL INFORMATION

Calories	370	Sugars	. . . . .3g
Protein	. . . . .10g	Fat	. . . . .19g
Carbohydrate	. . .39g	Saturates	. . . . . . .9g

 10–15 mins   30 mins

SERVES 4

I N G R E D I E N T S

2 tbsp butter

1 tbsp olive oil

1 onion, finely chopped

1 garlic clove, finely chopped

175 g/6 oz long-grain rice

400 ml/14 fl oz fish stock

175 g/6 oz skinless, boneless salmon fillet, chopped

85 g/3 oz smoked salmon, chopped

2 tbsp double cream

2 tbsp chopped fresh dill

3 spring onions, finely chopped

salt and pepper

lemon slices and fresh dill, to garnish

COOK'S TIP
Use smoked salmon trimmings for a budget dish.

1 Melt the butter with the oil in a large saucepan. Add the onion and cook gently for 10 minutes until softened but not coloured. Add the garlic and cook for a further 30 seconds.

2 Add the rice to the pan and cook for 2–3 minutes, stirring, until transparent. Add the fish stock and stir well. Bring to the boil, cover and simmer very gently for 10 minutes.

3 Add the salmon fillet and the smoked salmon and stir well, adding a little more stock or water if it seems dry. Return to the heat and cook a further 6–8 minutes until the fish and rice are tender and all the stock is absorbed.

4 Remove from the heat and stir in the cream, dill and spring onions. Season to taste and serve immediately, garnished with a sprig of dill and slice of lemon.

Jambalaya

Jambalaya is a dish of Cajun origin. There are as many versions of this dish as there are people who cook it. Here is a straightforward one.

NUTRITIONAL INFORMATION

Calories 283   Sugars 8g
Protein ....30g   Fat 14g
Carbohydrate ...12g   Saturates 3g

  20–25 mins   35 mins

SERVES 4

INGREDIENTS

2 tbsp vegetable oil

2 onions, roughly chopped

1 green pepper, deseeded and roughly chopped

2 celery sticks, roughly chopped

3 garlic cloves, finely chopped

2 tsp paprika

300 g/10½ oz skinless, boneless chicken breasts, chopped

100 g/3½ oz kabanos sausages, chopped

3 tomatoes, skinned and chopped

450 g/1 lb long-grain rice

850 ml/1½ pints hot chicken or fish stock

1 tsp dried oregano

2 fresh bay leaves

12 large prawn tails

4 spring onions, finely chopped

2 tbsp chopped fresh parsley

salt and pepper

salad, to serve

1 Heat the vegetable oil in a large frying pan and add the onions, pepper, celery and garlic. Cook for 8–10 minutes until all the vegetables have softened. Add the paprika and cook for a further 30 seconds. Add the chicken and sausages and cook for 8–10 minutes until lightly browned. Add the tomatoes and cook for 2–3 minutes until collapsed.

2 Add the rice to the pan and stir well. Pour in the hot stock, oregano and bay leaves and stir well. Cover and simmer for 10 minutes over a very low heat.

3 Add the prawns and stir well. Cover again and cook for a further 6–8 minutes until the rice is tender and the prawns are cooked through.

4 Stir in the spring onions, parsley and season to taste. Serve immediately.

COOK'S TIP

Jambalaya is a dish that has some basic ingredients – onions, green peppers, celery, rice and seasonings – to which you can add whatever you have to hand.

Prawn & Asparagus Risotto

An unusual and striking dish with fresh prawns and asparagus is very simple to prepare and ideal for impromptu supper parties.

NUTRITIONAL INFORMATION

Calories . . . . . . .566g Sugars 4g
Protein . . . . .30g Fat 14g
Carbohydrate . . .86g Saturates 2g

10–15 mins   45 mins

SERVES 4

I N G R E D I E N T S

1.2 litres/2 pints vegetable stock

350 g/12 oz asparagus, cut into 5-cm/2-inch lengths

2 tbsp olive oil

1 onion, finely chopped

1 garlic clove, finely chopped

350 g/12 oz arborio rice

450 g/1 lb raw tiger prawns, peeled and de-veined

2 tbsp olive paste or tapenade

2 tbsp chopped fresh basil

salt and pepper

Parmesan cheese, to garnish

1 Bring the vegetable stock to the boil in a large saucepan. Add the asparagus and cook for 3 minutes until just tender. Strain, reserving the stock, and refresh the asparagus under cold running water. Drain and set aside.

2 Heat the oil in a large frying pan, add the onion and cook for 5 minutes until softened. Add the garlic and cook for a further 30 seconds. Add the rice and stir for 1–2 minutes until coated with oil and slightly translucent.

3 Keep the stock on a low heat. Increase the heat under the rice to medium and begin adding the stock, a ladleful at a time, stirring well between additions. Continue until almost all the stock has been absorbed. This should take 20–25 minutes.

4 Add the prawns and asparagus, with the last ladleful of vegetable stock, and cook for a further 5 minutes until the prawns and rice are tender and the stock has been absorbed. Remove from the heat.

5 Stir in the olive paste, basil and seasoning and leave to stand for 1 minute. Serve immediately, garnished with Parmesan shavings.

Coconut Rice with Monkfish

A Thai-influenced dish of rice, cooked in coconut milk, with spicy grilled monkfish and fresh peas.

NUTRITIONAL INFORMATION

Calories 440   Sugars 8g
Protein ....22g   Fat 14g
Carbohydrate ...60g   Saturates 2g

10–15 mins, plus marinating time   45 mins

SERVES 4

INGREDIENTS

1 hot red chilli, deseeded and chopped

1 tsp crushed chilli flakes

2 garlic cloves, chopped

2 pinches saffron

3 tbsp roughly chopped mint leaves

4 tbsp olive oil

2 tbsp lemon juice

350 g/12 oz monkfish fillet, cut into bite-sized pieces

1 onion, finely chopped

225 g/8 oz long-grain rice

400 g/14 oz canned chopped tomatoes

200 ml/7 fl oz coconut milk

115 g/4 oz peas

salt and pepper

2 tbsp chopped fresh coriander, to garnish

1 In a food processor or blender, blend together the fresh and dried chilli, garlic, saffron, mint, olive oil and lemon juice until finely chopped but not smooth.

2 Put the monkfish into a non-metallic dish and pour over the spice paste, mixing together well. Set aside for 20 minutes to marinate.

3 Heat a large saucepan until it is very hot. Using a slotted spoon, lift the monkfish from the marinade and add, in batches, to the hot pan. Cook for 3–4 minutes until it is browned and firm. Remove with a slotted spoon and set aside while you cook the rice.

4 Add the onion and remaining marinade to the same pan and cook for 5 minutes until softened and lightly browned. Add the rice and stir until well coated. Add the tomatoes and coconut milk. Bring to the boil, cover and simmer very gently for 15 minutes. Stir in the peas, season, and arrange the fish over the top. Cover with foil and continue to cook over a very low heat for 5 minutes. Serve garnished with the chopped coriander.

Moules Marinières

The Spanish, French and Italians all serve variations of this simple mussel recipe, which is universally popular. Use the freshest mussels you can find.

NUTRITIONAL INFORMATION	
Calories 278	Sugars 6g
Protein 18g	Fat 14g
Carbohydrate ...10g	Saturates 2g

30 mins   25 mins

SERVES 4

INGREDIENTS

2 kg/4 lb 8 oz live mussels

4 tbsp olive oil

4–6 large garlic cloves, halved

800 g/28 oz canned chopped tomatoes

300 ml/10 fl oz dry white wine

2 tbsp finely chopped fresh flat-leaved parsley, plus extra for garnishing

1 tbsp finely chopped fresh oregano

salt and pepper

French bread, to serve

1 Leave the mussels to soak in a bowl of lightly salted water for 30 minutes. Rinse them under cold running water and lightly scrub to remove any sand from the shells. Using a small, sharp knife, remove the 'beards' from the shells.

2 Discard any broken mussels or open mussels that do not shut when tapped firmly with the back of a knife. This indicates they are dead and could cause food poisoning if eaten. Rinse the mussels again, then set aside in a colander.

3 Heat the olive oil in a large saucepan or stockpot over a medium-high heat. Add the garlic and fry, stirring, for about 3 minutes to flavour the oil. Using a slotted spoon, remove the garlic from the pan.

4 Add the tomatoes and their juice, the wine, parsley and oregano and bring to the boil, stirring. Lower the heat, cover and simmer for 5 minutes to allow the flavours to blend.

5 Add the mussels, cover and simmer for 5–8 minutes, shaking the pan regularly, until they open. Using a slotted spoon, transfer them to serving bowls, discarding any that are not open.

6 Season the sauce with salt and pepper to taste. Ladle the sauce over the mussels, sprinkle with extra parsley and serve at once with plenty of French bread to mop up the delicious juices.

Baked Cod with Curry

An easy, economical main dish that transforms a plain piece of fish into an exotic meal – try it with other white fish, too, such as monkfish.

NUTRITIONAL INFORMATION

Calories . . . . . . .223 Sugars 1g
Protein . . . . .31g Fat 4g
Carbohydrate . . .16g Saturates 0.1g

 20 mins   35–40 mins

SERVES 4

I N G R E D I E N T S

½ tsp sesame oil

4 pieces cod fillet, about 150 g/5½ oz each

85 g/3 oz fresh white breadcrumbs

2 tbsp blanched almonds, chopped

2 tsp Thai green curry paste

rind of ½ lime, finely grated

salt and pepper

lime slices and rind, and mixed green
  leaves, to garnish

boiled new potatoes, to serve

1 Brush the oil over the base of a wide, shallow ovenproof dish or tin, then put in the pieces of cod in a single layer.

2 Mix the fresh breadcrumbs, almonds, green curry paste and grated lime rind together, stirring well to blend thoroughly and evenly. Season to taste with salt and pepper.

3 Carefully spoon the crumb mixture over the fish pieces, pressing lightly to hold it in place.

4 Place the dish, uncovered, in a preheated oven at 200°C/400°F/ Gas Mark 6 and bake for 35–40 minutes until the fish is cooked through and the crumb topping is golden brown.

5 Serve hot, garnished with lime slices and rind and mixed green leaves, and accompanied by boiled new potatoes.

COOK'S TIP

To test whether the fish is cooked through, use a fork to pierce it in the thickest part – if the flesh is white all the way through and flakes apart easily, it is cooked sufficiently.

Fried Fish with Soy Sauce

This impressive dish is worth cooking for a special dinner, as it really is a talking point. Buy a very fresh whole fish on the day you plan to cook it.

NUTRITIONAL INFORMATION

Calories 290   Sugars 7g
Protein . . . . .27g   Fat 11g
Carbohydrate . . .23g   Saturates 1g

15–20 mins   20 mins

SERVES 4-6

INGREDIENTS

6 dried Chinese mushrooms

3 tbsp rice vinegar

2 tbsp soft light brown sugar

3 tbsp dark soy sauce

7.5-cm/3-inch piece fresh ginger root, finely chopped

4 spring onions, sliced diagonally

2 tsp cornflour

2 tbsp lime juice

1 sea bass, about 1 kg/2 lb 4 oz, cleaned

4 tbsp plain flour

sunflower oil for deep-frying

salt and pepper

shredded Chinese leaves and radish slices, to serve

1 radish, sliced but left whole, to garnish

1 Soak the dried mushrooms in hot water for about 10 minutes, then drain well, reserving 100 ml/3½ fl oz of the liquid. Cut the mushrooms into thin slices.

2 Mix the reserved mushroom liquid with the rice vinegar, sugar and soy sauce. Place in a saucepan with the mushrooms and bring to the boil. Reduce the heat and simmer for 3–4 minutes.

3 Add the ginger and spring onions and simmer for 1 minute. Stir the cornflour and lime juice into the pan and cook for 1–2 minutes until the sauce thickens and clears. Keep the sauce to one side.

4 Season the fish inside and out with salt and pepper, then dust lightly with flour, shaking off the excess.

5 Heat 2.5 cm/1inch of oil in a wide pan to 190°C/375°F, or until a cube of bread browns in 30 seconds. Carefully lower the fish into the oil and fry on each side for about 3–4 minutes until golden.

6 Lift the fish out of the pan, draining off the excess oil, and place on a serving plate. Heat the sauce until boiling, then spoon it over the fish. Serve immediately, surrounded by shredded Chinese leaves and sliced radishes, garnished with the sliced whole radish.

Tuna in Sweet-&-Sour Sauce

Tuna is a firm, meaty-textured fish. You can also use shark or mackerel with this rich sweet-and-sour sauce.

NUTRITIONAL INFORMATION

Calories	303	Sugars	........12g
Protein	........31g	Fat	..........12g
Carbohydrate	...20g	Saturates	.......3g

 30 mins   20 mins

SERVES 4

INGREDIENTS

4 fresh tuna steaks, about 500 g/
  1 lb 2 oz total weight

¼ tsp ground black pepper

2 tbsp groundnut oil

1 onion, diced

1 small red pepper, deseeded and cut
  into matchsticks

1 garlic clove, crushed

1 tbsp soft light brown sugar

½ cucumber, deseeded and cut
  into matchsticks

2 pineapple slices, diced

1 tsp fresh ginger root, finely chopped

1 tbsp cornflour

1½ tbsp lime juice

1 tbsp Thai fish sauce

250 ml/9 fl oz fish stock

lime and cucumber slices,
  to garnish

1 Sprinkle the tuna steaks with pepper on both sides. Heat a heavy frying pan or griddle and brush with a little of the oil. Put the tuna steaks in the pan and cook for about 8 minutes, turning them over once during cooking.

2 Heat the remaining oil in another pan and fry the onion, pepper and garlic gently for 3–4 minutes to soften.

3 Take off the heat and stir in the sugar, cucumber, pineapple and ginger.

4 Blend the cornflour with the lime juice and fish sauce, then stir into the stock and add to the pan. Stir over a medium heat until boiling, then cook for 1–2 minutes until thickened and clear.

5 Spoon the sweet-and-sour sauce over the tuna and serve garnished with lime slices and cucumber.

Thai-spiced Salmon

Marinated in delicate Thai spices and quickly pan-fried to perfection, these salmon fillets are ideal for a special dinner.

NUTRITIONAL INFORMATION

Calories 329	Sugars 0.1g
Protein 30g	Fat 23g
Carbohydrate . . .0.1g	Saturates 4g

20 mins, plus refrigeration time

5 mins

SERVES 4

I N G R E D I E N T S

2.5-cm/1-inch piece fresh ginger root, grated

1 tsp coriander seeds, crushed

¼ tsp chilli powder

1 tbsp lime juice

1 tsp sesame oil

4 pieces salmon fillet with skin, about 150 g/5½ oz each

2 tbsp vegetable oil

boiled rice and stir-fried vegetables, to serve

1 In a bowl, mix together the ginger, coriander, chilli powder, lime juice and sesame oil.

2 Place the salmon on a wide, non-metallic plate or dish and spoon the mixture over the flesh side of the fillets, spreading it out to coat each piece of salmon evenly.

3 Cover the dish with cling film and chill the salmon in the refrigerator for about 30 minutes.

4 Heat a wide, heavy-based frying pan or griddle pan with the oil over a high heat. Place the salmon on the hot pan or griddle, skin side down.

5 Cook the fish for 4–5 minutes, without turning, until the salmon is crusty underneath and the flesh flakes easily. Serve at once with the boiled rice and stir-fried vegetables.

COOK'S TIP

It's important to use a heavy-based pan or solid griddle for this recipe, so that the fish cooks evenly throughout without sticking. If the fish is very thick, you may prefer to turn it over carefully to cook on the other side for 2–3 minutes.

Scallops with Lime & Chilli

Really fresh scallops have a delicate flavour and texture, needing only minimal cooking, as in this simple stir-fry.

NUTRITIONAL INFORMATION

Calories 145	Sugars 1g	
Protein 17g	Fat 7g	
Carbohydrate 4g	Saturates 3g	

🍞 🍞 🍞

30 mins   🕐 10 mins

SERVES 4

INGREDIENTS

16 large scallops

1 tbsp butter

1 tbsp vegetable oil

1 tsp garlic, crushed

1 tsp fresh ginger root, grated

1 bunch spring onions, finely sliced

rind of 1 kaffir lime, finely grated

1 small red chilli, deseeded and very finely chopped

3 tbsp kaffir lime juice

salt and pepper

lime wedges and boiled rice, to serve

COOK'S TIP

Frozen scallops can be used, but make sure they are thoroughly defrosted before you cook them. Drain off all excess moisture and pat dry with kitchen paper.

1 Trim the scallops to remove any black intestine, then wash and pat dry. Separate the corals from the white parts, then horizontally slice each white part in half, making 2 rounds.

2 Heat the butter and oil in a frying pan or wok. Add the garlic and ginger and stir-fry for 1 minute without browning. Add the spring onions and stir-fry for a further minute.

3 Add the scallops and continue stir-frying over a high heat for 4–5 minutes. Stir in the lime rind, chilli and lime juice and cook for a further minute.

4 Serve the scallops hot, with the juices spooned over them, accompanied by lime wedges and boiled rice.

Goan Fish Curry

Goan cuisine is famous for its seafood and for its vindaloo dishes, which tend to be very hot. This recipe is mildly spiced, but very flavourful.

NUTRITIONAL INFORMATION

Calories 302   Sugars 7g
Protein . . . . .31g   Fat 17g
Carbohydrate . . . .8g   Saturates 7g

20 mins   15 mins

SERVES 4

INGREDIENTS

675 g/1½ lb monkfish fillet, cut into chunks

1 tbsp cider vinegar

1 tsp salt

1 tsp ground turmeric

3 tbsp vegetable oil

2 garlic cloves, crushed

1 small onion, finely chopped

2 tsp ground coriander

1 tsp cayenne pepper

2 tsp paprika

2 tbsp tamarind pulp plus 2 tbsp boiling water (see method)

85 g/3 oz creamed coconut, cut into pieces

300 ml/10 fl oz warm water

plain boiled rice, to serve

1 Put the fish on a plate and drizzle the vinegar over it. Mix together half the salt and half the turmeric and sprinkle evenly over the fish. Cover and set aside for about 20 minutes.

2 Heat the oil in a frying pan and add the garlic. Brown slightly then add the onion and fry for 3–4 minutes until soft, but not browned. Add the ground coriander and stir for 1 minute.

3 Mix the remaining turmeric, cayenne and paprika with about 2 tablespoons water to make a paste. Add this to the pan and cook over a low heat for 1–2 minutes.

4 Mix the tamarind pulp with the 2 tablespoons boiling water and stir well. When the water appears thick and the pulp has come away from the seeds, pass this mixture through a sieve, rubbing the pulp well. Discard the seeds once you have finished.

5 Add the creamed coconut, warm water and tamarind paste to the pan and stir until the coconut has dissolved. Add the pieces of fish and any juices on the plate and simmer gently for 4–5 minutes until the sauce has thickened and the fish is just tender. Serve the curry immediately on a bed of plain boiled rice.

Mackerel Escabeche

Although the word *escabeche* is Spanish, variations of this dish are cooked all over the Mediterranean.

NUTRITIONAL INFORMATION

Calories ....750 Sugars 3g
Protein ....33g Fat 63g
Carbohydrate ...12g Saturates 11g

 10 mins 15 mins

SERVES 4

INGREDIENTS

150 ml/5 fl oz olive oil

4 mackerel, filleted

2 tbsp seasoned flour, for dusting

4 tbsp red wine vinegar

1 onion, finely sliced

1 strip orange rind, removed with a
   potato peeler

1 sprig fresh thyme

1 sprig fresh rosemary

1 fresh bay leaf

4 garlic cloves, crushed

2 fresh red chillies, bruised

1 tsp salt

3 tbsp chopped fresh flat-leaved parsley

crusty bread, to serve

1 Heat half the oil in a frying pan and dust the mackerel fillets with the seasoned flour.

2 Add the fish to the frying pan and cook for about 30 seconds each side until almost cooked through.

3 Transfer the mackerel to a shallow dish, large enough to hold the fillets in a single layer.

4 Add the the vinegar, onion, orange rind, thyme, rosemary, bay leaf, garlic, chillies and salt to the pan. Simmer for 10 minutes.

5 Add the remaining olive oil and the chopped parsley. Pour the mixture over the fish and leave until cold. Serve with plenty of crusty bread.

VARIATION

Substitute 12 whole sardines, cleaned, with heads removed. Cook in the same way. Tuna steaks are also delicious served like this.

Haddock Baked in Yogurt

This is a very simple dish using storecupboard ingredients, but the interesting blend of spices lifts it out of the ordinary.

NUTRITIONAL INFORMATION

Calories . . . . . . .448g Sugars 16g
Protein . . . . .47g Fat 21g
Carbohydrate . . .20g Saturates 8g

15 mins   45 mins

SERVES 4

I N G R E D I E N T S

2 large onions, thinly sliced

900 g/2 lb haddock fillet, from the head end

425 ml/15 fl oz natural yogurt

2 tbsp lemon juice

1 tsp sugar

2 tsp ground cumin

2 tsp ground coriander

pinch garam masala

pinch cayenne pepper, to taste

1 tsp freshly grated ginger root

3 tbsp vegetable oil

4 tbsp cold unsalted butter, cut into pieces

salt and pepper

1 Line a large baking dish with the onion slices. Cut the fish into strips widthways and lay the fish in a single layer over the onions.

2 Mix together the yogurt, lemon juice, sugar, cumin, coriander, garam masala, cayenne, ginger, oil and seasoning. Pour this sauce over the fish, making sure it goes under it as well. Cover tightly.

3 Bake the dish in a preheated oven at 190°C/375°F/Gas Mark 5 for 30 minutes or until the fish is just tender.

4 Carefully pour the sauce off the fish into a saucepan. Bring to the boil and simmer to reduce the sauce to about 350 ml/12 fl oz. Remove from the heat.

5 Add the cubes of butter to the sauce and whisk until melted and incorporated. Pour the sauce back over the fish and serve.

COOK'S TIP

When you pour the sauce off the fish it will look thin and separated, but reducing and stirring in the butter will help to amalgamate it.

Cod Italienne

Not strictly authentic, but this dish uses the typical Italian ingredients of tomatoes, capers, olives and basil to make a delicious supper dish.

NUTRITIONAL INFORMATION

Calories 387	Sugars 8g
Protein 44g	Fat 16g
Carbohydrate . . .10g	Saturates 6g

 20 mins   1hr 30 mins

SERVES 4

INGREDIENTS

2 tbsp olive oil

1 onion, finely chopped

2 garlic cloves, finely chopped

2 tsp freshly chopped thyme

150 ml/5 fl oz red wine

800 g/28 oz canned chopped tomatoes

pinch sugar

50 g/1¾ oz pitted black olives, roughly chopped

50 g/1¾ oz pitted green olives, roughly chopped

2 tbsp capers, drained, rinsed and roughly chopped

2 tbsp chopped fresh basil

4 cod steaks, each weighing about 175 g/6 oz

150 g/5½ oz buffalo mozzarella, drained and sliced

salt and pepper

buttered noodles, to serve

1 Heat the olive oil in a large saucepan. Add the onion and fry gently for 5 minutes until softened but not coloured. Add the garlic and thyme and cook a further minute.

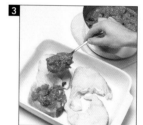

2 Add the red wine and increase the heat. Simmer until reduced and syrupy. Add the tomatoes and sugar and bring to the boil. Cover and simmer for 30 minutes. Uncover and simmer a further 20 minutes until thick. Stir in the olives, capers and basil. Season to taste.

3 Arrange the cod steaks in a shallow ovenproof dish (a lasagne dish is perfect) and spoon the tomato sauce over the top. Bake in a preheated oven at 190°C/375°F/Gas Mark 5 for 20–25 minutes, until the fish is just tender.

4 Remove the dish from the oven and arrange the mozzarella slices on top of the fish.

5 Return the cod to the oven for a further 5–10 minutes until the cheese has melted. Serve immediately with buttered noodles.

Cotriade

This is a rich French stew of fish and vegetables, flavoured with saffron and herbs. The fish and vegetables, and the soup, are served separately.

NUTRITIONAL INFORMATION

Calories 81   Sugars 0.9g
Protein . . . . .7.4g   Fat 3.9g
Carbohydrate . . .3.8g   Saturates 1.1g

15 mins   40 mins

SERVES 6

I N G R E D I E N T S

large pinch saffron

600 ml/1 pint hot fish stock

1 tbsp olive oil

2 tbsp butter

1 onion, sliced

2 garlic cloves, chopped

1 leek, sliced

1 small fennel bulb, finely sliced

450 g/1 lb potatoes, cut into chunks

150 ml/5 fl oz dry white wine

1 tbsp fresh thyme leaves

2 bay leaves

4 ripe tomatoes, skinned and chopped

900g/2 lb mixed fish such as haddock, hake, mackerel, red or grey mullet, roughly chopped

2 tbsp chopped fresh parsley

salt and pepper

crusty bread, to serve

1 Using a mortar and pestle, crush the saffron and add to the fish stock. Stir the mixture and leave to infuse for at least 10 minutes.

2 In a large saucepan, heat the oil and butter together. Add the onion and cook gently for 4–5 minutes until softened. Add the garlic, leek, fennel and potatoes. Put a lid on the pan and cook for a further 10–15 minutes until the vegetables have softened.

3 Add the wine and simmer rapidly for 3–4 minutes until it has reduced by half. Add the thyme, bay leaves and tomatoes and stir well. Add the saffron-infused fish stock. Bring to the boil, cover and simmer gently for 15 minutes until the vegetables are tender.

4 Add the fish, return to the boil and simmer for a further 3–4 minutes until the fish is tender. Add the parsley and season to taste. Using a slotted spoon, remove the fish and vegetables to a warmed serving dish. Serve the soup with plenty of crusty bread.

Moroccan Fish Tagine

A tagine is an earthenware cooking dish that has a domed lid with a steam hole in it. However, this recipe can be made in an ordinary pan.

NUTRITIONAL INFORMATION

Calories 188	Sugars 5g	
Protein 17g	Fat 11g	
Carbohydrate 7g	Saturates 1g	

 20 mins   🕐 1 hr 30 mins

SERVES 4

INGREDIENTS

2 tbsp olive oil

1 large onion, finely chopped

large pinch saffron strands

½ tsp ground cinnamon

1 tsp ground coriander

½ tsp ground cumin

½ tsp ground turmeric

200 g/7 oz canned chopped tomatoes

300 ml/10 fl oz fish stock

4 small red mullet, cleaned, boned and heads and tails removed

50 g/1¾ oz pitted green olives

1 tbsp chopped preserved lemon

3 tbsp fresh chopped coriander

salt and pepper

couscous, to serve

 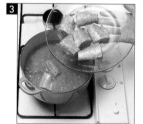 

1 Heat the olive oil in a large saucepan or flameproof casserole. Add the onion and cook gently for 10 minutes without colouring until softened. Add the saffron, cinnamon, coriander, cumin and turmeric and cook for a further 30 seconds, stirring.

2 Add the chopped tomatoes and fish stock and stir well. Bring to the boil, cover and simmer for 15 minutes. Uncover and simmer for a further 20–35 minutes until the sauce has thickened.

3 Cut each red mullet in half then add the pieces to the pan, pushing them into the sauce. Simmer gently for a further 5–6 minutes until the fish is just cooked.

4 Carefully stir in the olives, preserved lemon and the chopped coriander. Season to taste and serve with couscous.

COOK'S TIP

To make preserved lemons, take enough lemons to fill a preserving jar and quarter them lengthways without cutting all the way through. Pack the jar of lemons with 50 g/1¾ oz sea salt per lemon. Add the juice of a further lemon and top up with water to cover. Leave for at least 1 month before using.

Spicy Prawns with Courgettes

The best way to approach this recipe is to prepare things beforehand – including measuring out the spices. The cooking time is then very quick.

NUTRITIONAL INFORMATION

Calories ....272 Sugars 5g
Protein ....29g Fat 15g
Carbohydrate ....5g Saturates 2g

20 mins   15 mins

SERVES 4

INGREDIENTS

350 g/12 oz small courgettes

1 tsp salt

450 g/1 lb cooked tiger prawns

5 tbsp vegetable oil

4 garlic cloves, finely chopped

5 tbsp chopped fresh coriander

1 fresh green chilli, deseeded and
    finely chopped

½ tsp ground turmeric

1½ tsp ground cumin

pinch cayenne pepper

200 g/7 oz canned chopped tomatoes

1 tsp freshly grated ginger root

1 tbsp lemon juice

steamed basmati rice, to serve

1 Wash and trim the courgettes. Cut them into small batons and put into a colander, and then sprinkle with a little of the salt. Set aside for 30 minutes. Rinse, drain and pat dry. Spread the prawns on kitchen paper to drain.

2 In a wok or frying pan, heat the oil over a high heat. Add the garlic. As soon as the garlic begins to brown, add the courgettes, coriander, green chilli, turmeric, cumin, cayenne, tomatoes, ginger, lemon juice and remaining salt. Stir well and bring to the boil.

3 Cover and simmer over a low heat for about 5 minutes. Uncover and add the prawns.

4 Increase the heat to high and simmer for about 5 minutes to reduce the liquid to a thick sauce. Serve immediately with steamed basmati rice, garnished with lime wedges.

VARIATION

If you can't find cooked tiger prawns for this recipe, use cooked peeled prawns instead, but these release quite a lot of liquid so you may need to increase the final simmering time to thicken the sauce.

Poached Rainbow Trout

This colourful, flavoursome dish is served cold and therefore makes a lovely summer lunch or supper dish.

NUTRITIONAL INFORMATION

Calories 99	Sugars 1.1g	
Protein 5.7g	Fat 6.3g	
Carbohydrate . . .3.7g	Saturates 1g	

🥘 10 mins 🕐 1 hr 5 mins

SERVES 4

INGREDIENTS

1.3 kg/3 lb rainbow trout fillet, cleaned

700 g/1 lb 9 oz new potatoes

3 spring onions, finely chopped

1 egg, hard-boiled and chopped

COURT-BOUILLON

850 ml/1½ pints cold water

850 ml/1½ pints dry white wine

3 tbsp white wine vinegar

2 large carrots, roughly chopped

1 onion, roughly chopped

2 celery sticks, roughly chopped

2 leeks, roughly chopped

2 garlic cloves, roughly chopped

2 fresh bay leaves

4 sprigs fresh parsley

4 sprigs fresh thyme

6 black peppercorns

1 tsp salt

WATERCRESS MAYONNAISE

1 egg yolk

1 tsp Dijon mustard

1 tsp white wine vinegar

55g/2 oz watercress leaves, chopped

225 ml/8 fl oz light olive oil

salt and pepper

1 Put all the court-bouillon ingredients in a large pan, cover and simmer for 30 minutes. Strain through a fine sieve into a clean pan. Bring to the boil and simmer fast, uncovered, for 15–20 minutes until reduced to 600 ml/1 pint.

2 Place the trout in a frying pan. Add the court-bouillon and bring slowly to the boil. Remove from the heat and leave in the poaching liquid to go cold.

3 Make the watercress mayonnaise. Put the egg yolk, mustard, vinegar, watercress and seasoning into a food processor and blend for 30 seconds until foaming. Add olive oil, drop by drop, until the mixture begins to thicken. Continue adding the oil in a slow stream until incorporated. Add a little hot water if too thick. Season and set aside.

4 Cook the potatoes in boiling water for 12–15 minutes. Drain and refresh under cold running water. Set aside.

5 Toss the cold potatoes with the watercress mayonnaise, spring onions and hard-boiled egg.

6 Lift the fish from the poaching liquid and drain on kitchen paper. Carefully pull the skin away from each trout. Serve the fish immediately with the potato salad.

Hake Steaks with Chermoula

The cooking time may seem long and indeed you could decrease it slightly if you prefer, but in Morocco they like their fish well cooked.

NUTRITIONAL INFORMATION

Calories	590	Sugars	.........1g
Protein	........42g	Fat	..........46g
Carbohydrate	....2g	Saturates	.......7g

 10 mins, plus marinating time

 35–40 mins

SERVES 4

I N G R E D I E N T S

4 hake steaks, about 225 g/8 oz each

115 g/4 oz pitted green olives

M A R I N A D E

6 tbsp finely chopped fresh coriander

6 tbsp finely chopped fresh parsley

6 garlic cloves, crushed

1 tbsp ground cumin

1 tsp ground coriander

1 tbsp paprika

pinch cayenne pepper

150 ml/5 fl oz fresh lemon juice

300 ml/10 fl oz olive oil

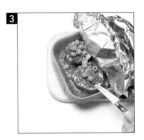

1 For the marinade, mix together the fresh coriander, parsley, garlic, cumin, coriander, paprika, cayenne, lemon juice and olive oil.

2 Wash and dry the hake steaks and place in an ovenproof dish. Pour the marinade over the fish and leave for at least 1 hour and preferably overnight.

3 Before cooking the hake stake, scatter the green olives over the fish. Cover the dish with foil.

4 Place the hake in a preheated oven at 160°C/325°F/Gas Mark 3. Cook for about 35–40 minutes until the fish is tender. Serve the steaks with freshly cooked vegetables.

VARIATION

Remove the fish from the marinade and dust with seasoned flour. Fry in oil or clarified butter until golden. Warm through the marinade, but do not boil, and serve as a sauce with lemon slices.

Stuffed Mackerel

This is a variation of a Middle Eastern recipe for stuffed mackerel, which involves removing the mackerel flesh while leaving the skin intact.

NUTRITIONAL INFORMATION

Calories 488	Sugars 12g
Protein 34g	Fat 34g
Carbohydrate ...12g	Saturates 6g

15 mins   45 mins

SERVES 4

INGREDIENTS

4 large mackerel, cleaned

1 tbsp olive oil

1 small onion, finely sliced

1 tsp ground cinnamon

½ tsp ground ginger

2 tbsp raisins

2 tbsp pine kernels, toasted

8 vine leaves in brine, drained

salt and pepper

1 Wash and dry the mackerel and set aside. Heat the olive oil in a small frying pan and add the onion. Cook gently for about 5 minutes until the onion is softened. Add the cinnamon and ginger and cook for 30 seconds before adding the raisins and pine kernels. Remove the mixture from the heat and allow it to cool.

2 Stuff each fish with a quarter of the stuffing mixture. Wrap each fish in 2 vine leaves, securing with cocktail sticks.

3 Cook on a preheated barbecue or ridged grill pan for 5 minutes on each side until the vine leaves have scorched and the fish is tender. Serve immediately.

VARIATION

This stuffing works equally well with many other fish, including sea bass and red mullet.

Skate with Black Butter

Skate has a strong flavour that makes it a rich fish. It is therefore perfect partnered with this sauce, which is sharp in flavour.

NUTRITIONAL INFORMATION

Calories 381	Sugars 0g	
Protein 34g	Fat 27g	
Carbohydrate 0g	Saturates 17g	

20 mins

1 hr 30 mins

SERVES 4

I N G R E D I E N T S

900 g/2 lb skate wings, cut into 4

175 g/6 oz butter

50 ml/2 fl oz red wine vinegar

15 g/½ oz capers, drained

1 tbsp chopped fresh parsley

salt and pepper

C O U R T - B O U I L L O N

850 ml/1½ pints cold water

850 ml/1½ pints dry white wine

3 tbsp white wine vinegar

2 large carrots, roughly chopped

1 onion, roughly chopped

2 celery sticks, roughly chopped

2 leeks, roughly chopped

2 garlic cloves, roughly chopped

2 fresh bay leaves

4 parsley sprigs

4 thyme sprigs

6 black peppercorns

1 tsp salt

T O   S E R V E

new potatoes

green vegetable

1 Begin by making the court-bouillon. Put all of the ingredients into a large saucepan and bring slowly to the boil. Cover and simmer gently for 30 minutes. Strain the liquid through a fine sieve into a clean pan. Bring to the boil again and simmer fast, uncovered, for 15–20 minutes, until reduced to 600 ml/1 pint.

2 Place the skate in a wide shallow pan and pour the court-bouillon over it. Bring to the boil and simmer very gently for 15 minutes, or a little longer depending on the thickness of the skate. Drain the fish and put to one side, keeping it warm.

3 Meanwhile, melt the butter in a frying pan. Cook over a medium heat until the butter changes colour to a dark brown and smells very nutty.

4 Add the vinegar, capers and parsley and allow to simmer for 1 minute. Season to taste with salt and pepper. Pour over the fish. Serve immediately with plenty of boiled new potatoes and a seasonal fresh green vegetable of your choice.

Dover Sole à la Meunière

Dover sole à la Meunière, or 'in the style of a miller's wife', gets its name from the light dusting of flour that the fish is given before frying.

NUTRITIONAL INFORMATION

Calories	584	Sugars	.........0g
Protein	........74g	Fat	..........29g
Carbohydrate	...10g	Saturates	......14g

 20 mins   15 mins

SERVES 4

INGREDIENTS

4 tbsp plain flour

1 tsp salt

4 x 400-g/14-oz Dover soles, cleaned and skinned

150 g/5½ oz butter

3 tbsp lemon juice

1 tbsp chopped fresh parsley

¼ of a preserved lemon, finely chopped (optional)

salt and pepper

lemon wedges, to garnish

1 Mix the flour with the salt and place on a large plate or tray. Drop the fish into the flour, one at a time, and shake well to remove any excess. Melt 40 g/ 1½ oz (3 tablespoons) of the butter in a small saucepan and use to brush the fish liberally all over.

2 Place the fish under a preheated hot grill and cook for 5 minutes each side.

3 Meanwhile, melt the remaining butter in a pan. Pour cold water into a bowl, large enough to take the base of the pan. Keep nearby.

4 Heat the butter until it turns a golden brown and begins to smell nutty.

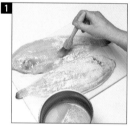

Remove immediately from the heat and immerse the base of the pan in the cold water, to arrest cooking.

5 Put the fish on to individual serving plates, drizzle with the lemon juice and sprinkle with the parsley and preserved lemon, if using. Pour over the browned butter and serve immediately, garnished with lemon wedges.

COOK'S TIP

If you have a large enough pan (or two) you can fry the floured fish in butter, if you prefer.

Sea Bass with Ratatouille

Sea bass has a delightful taste and texture. Here it is cooked simply and served with a highly flavoured ratatouille.

NUTRITIONAL INFORMATION

Calories . . . . . . .373g   Sugars 9g
Protein . . . . .42g   Fat 18g
Carbohydrate . . .10g   Saturates 3g

30 mins   1hr 5 mins

SERVES 4

I N G R E D I E N T S

2 large sea bass, filleted

olive oil, for brushing

salt and pepper

R A T A T O U I L L E

1 large aubergine

2 medium courgettes

1 tbsp sea salt

4 tbsp olive oil

1 medium onion, roughly chopped

2 garlic cloves, crushed

½ red pepper, deseeded and
   roughly chopped

½ green pepper, deseeded and
   roughly chopped

2 large ripe tomatoes, skinned and chopped

1 tbsp freshly chopped basil

D R E S S I N G

5 tbsp roughly chopped fresh basil

2 garlic cloves, roughly chopped

4 tbsp olive oil

1 tbsp lemon juice

salt and pepper

1 To make the ratatouille, chop the aubergine and courgette. Sprinkle with the salt and leave for 30 minutes. Rinse and pat dry on kitchen paper.

2 Heat the oil in a large saucepan and add the onion and garlic. Cook gently for 10 minutes until softened. Add the peppers, aubergine and courgette. Season and stir well. Cover and simmer very gently for 30 minutes until all the vegetables have softened. Add the tomatoes and cook for a further 15 minutes.

3 Meanwhile make the dressing. Put the basil, garlic and half the olive oil into a food processor and blend. Add the remaining olive oil, lemon juice and seasoning.

4 Season the sea bass fillets and brush with a little oil. Preheat a frying pan until very hot and add the fish, skin side down. Cook for 2–3 minutes until the skin is browned and crispy. Turn the fish and cook for a further 2–3 minutes until just cooked through.

5 To serve, stir the basil into the ratatouille then divide between 4 serving plates. Top with the fresh fried fish and spoon the dressing around it.

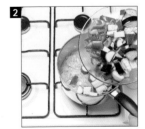

Whole Sea Bass with Ginger

This is a lovely oriental-inspired dish of sea bass, delicately flavoured with spring onions, ginger and soy sauce.

NUTRITIONAL INFORMATION

Calories 185	Sugars 1g	
Protein 31g	Fat 6g	
Carbohydrate 2g	Saturates 1g	

20 mins   10–12 mins

SERVES 4

INGREDIENTS

800 g/1 lb 12 oz whole sea bass, cleaned and scaled

4 tbsp light soy sauce

5 spring onions, cut into long, fine shreds

2 tbsp finely shredded fresh ginger root

4 tbsp fresh coriander leaves

5 tsp sunflower oil

1 tsp sesame oil

4 tbsp hot fish stock

steamed rice, to serve

lime wedges, to garnish

1 Wash and dry the fish. Brush with 2 tablespoons of the soy sauce. The fish is cooked in a steamer. Scatter half the spring onions and all the ginger over a steaming tray or large plate and put the fish on top.

2 Half-fill a large saucepan with water and fit a steamer on top. Bring the water to the boil. Put the steaming plate with the sea bass into the steamer and cover with a tight-fitting lid. Keeping the water boiling, steam the fish for 10–12 minutes until tender.

3 Carefully remove the plate and lift the fish on to a serving platter, leaving behind the spring onions and ginger. Scatter the remaining spring onions and coriander leaves over the top.

4 Put the sunflower oil into a small saucepan and heat until almost smoking. Add the sesame oil and immediately pour over the fish and spring onions. Mix the remaining soy sauce with the fish stock and pour this over the fish. Serve immediately with steamed rice and garnish with lime wedges.

Stuffed Monkfish Tail

A very impressive-looking dish, which is very simple to prepare. The fish is stuffed with herbs and wrapped in slices of ham.

NUTRITIONAL INFORMATION

Calories 154   Sugars 0g
Protein . . . . .24g   Fat 6g
Carbohydrate . . . .0g   Saturates 1g

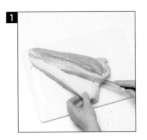

15 mins   40 mins

SERVES 6

I N G R E D I E N T S

750 g/1 lb 10 oz monkfish tail, skinned and trimmed

6 slices Parma ham

4 tbsp chopped mixed herbs such as parsley, chives, basil, sage

1 tsp finely grated lemon rind

2 tbsp olive oil

salt and pepper

TO SERVE

shredded stir-fried vegetables

new potatoes

1 Using a sharp knife, carefully cut down each side of the central bone of the monkfish to leave 2 fillets. Wash and dry the fillets.

2 Lay the Parma ham slices widthways on a clean work surface so that they overlap slightly. Lay the fish fillets lengthways on top of the ham so that the two cut sides face each other.

3 Mix together the chopped herbs and the grated lemon rind. Season well. Pack this mixture onto the cut surface of one monkfish fillet. Press the 2 fillets together and wrap them tightly with the Parma ham slices. Secure the package with string or cocktail sticks.

4 Heat the olive oil in a large ovenproof frying pan and place the fish in the pan, seam-side down first, and brown the wrapped monkfish tail all over.

5 Transfer the pan to an oven preheated to 200°C/400°F/Gas Mark 6, and bake for 25 minutes until golden and the fish is tender. Remove from the oven and allow to rest for 10 minutes before cutting the fillets into thick slices. Serve the fish slices with shredded stir-fried vegetables and new potatoes.

COOK'S TIP

It is possible to remove the central bone from a monkfish tail without separating the two fillets completely. This makes it easier to stuff, but takes some practice.

Seared Tuna Steaks

Meaty tuna steaks have enough flavour to stand up to the robust taste of anchovies. Serve this with pan-fried potatoes or a mixed rice dish.

NUTRITIONAL INFORMATION

Calories 564	Sugars 0g
Protein 55g	Fat 38g
Carbohydrate 0g	Saturates 19g

🧊 35 mins   🕐 5 mins

SERVES 4

INGREDIENTS

olive oil

4 thick tuna steaks, each about
225 g/8 oz and 2 cm/¾ inch thick

salt and pepper

ANCHOVY AND ORANGE BUTTER

8 anchovy fillets in oil, drained

4 spring onions, finely chopped

1 tbsp finely grated orange rind

115 g/4 oz unsalted butter

¼ tsp lemon juice

pepper

TO GARNISH

fresh flat-leaved parsley sprigs

orange rind strips

1 To make the anchovy and orange butter, very finely chop the anchovies and put them in a bowl with the spring onions, orange rind and softened butter. Beat until all the ingredients are blended together, seasoning with lemon juice and pepper to taste.

2 Place the flavoured butter on a sheet of baking parchment and roll it up into a log shape. Carefully fold over the ends of the paper and then place the butter in the freezer for about 15 minutes to become firm.

3 To cook the tuna, heat a ridged frying pan over a high heat. Lightly brush the pan with olive oil, add the tuna steaks, in batches if necessary, and fry for 2 minutes. Turn the steaks over and fry for 2 minutes for rare, or up to 4 minutes for well done. Season to taste with salt and pepper.

4 Transfer the fish to a warm plate and put 2 thin slices of anchovy butter on each of the tuna steaks. Garnish with fresh parsley sprigs and orange rind and serve at once.

VARIATION
If you particularly like hot, spicy food, add a pinch of dried chilli flakes to the butter mixture.

Swordfish à la Maltaise

The firm texture of swordfish means it is often simply grilled, but it also lends itself to this delicate technique of cooking in a paper parcel.

NUTRITIONAL INFORMATION

Calories	303	Sugars	........10g
Protein	........34g	Fat	.........13g
Carbohydrate	...13g	Saturates	.......3g

 35 mins   30 mins

SERVES 4

INGREDIENTS

1 tbsp fennel seeds

2 tbsp fruity extra-virgin olive oil, plus extra for brushing and drizzling

2 large onions, thinly sliced

1 small garlic clove, crushed

4 swordfish steaks, about 175 g/6 oz each

1 large lemon, cut in half

2 large sun-ripened tomatoes, finely chopped

4 sprigs fresh thyme

salt and pepper

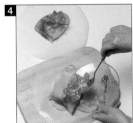

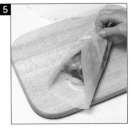

1 Place the fennel seeds in a dry frying pan over a medium-high heat and toast, stirring, until they give off their aroma, watching carefully that they do not burn. Immediately tip out of the pan on to a plate. Set aside.

2 Heat 2 tablespoons of the olive oil in the pan. Add the onions and fry for 5 minutes, stirring occasionally. Add the garlic and continue frying the onions until very soft and tender, but not brown. Remove the pan from the heat.

3 Cut out four 30-cm/12-inch circles of baking parchment. Very lightly brush the centre of each paper circle with olive oil. Divide the onions between the circles, flattening them out to about the size of the fish steaks.

4 Top the onions in each parcel with a swordfish steak. Squeeze lemon juice over the fish steaks and drizzle with a little olive oil. Scatter the tomatoes over the top, add a sprig of thyme to each and season with salt and pepper to taste.

5 Fold the edges of the baking parchment together, scrunching them tightly so that no cooking juices escape during cooking. Place the paper parcels on a baking sheet and cook them in a preheated oven at 200°C/400°F/Gas Mark 6 for 20 minutes.

6 To test if the fish is cooked, open one package and pierce the flesh with a knife – it should flake easily. Serve straight from the paper packages.

Wrapped Red Mullet

Fresh thyme, which grows wild throughout the Mediterranean, flavours this rustic dish. Serve with boiled new potatoes.

NUTRITIONAL INFORMATION

Calories	320	Sugars	.........8g
Protein	........37g	Fat	..........16g
Carbohydrate	....9g	Saturates	.......1g

25 mins   35 mins

SERVES 4

INGREDIENTS

3 tbsp olive oil, plus extra for rubbing

2 large red peppers, cored, deseeded and thinly sliced

2 large bulbs fennel, trimmed and thinly sliced

1 large clove garlic, crushed

8 sprigs fresh thyme, plus extra for garnishing

20–24 vine leaves in brine

1 lemon

4 red mullet, about 225 g/8 oz each, scaled and gutted

salt and pepper

1 Heat the oil in a large frying pan over a medium–low heat. Add the peppers, fennel, garlic and 4 sprigs of thyme and stir together. Cook, stirring occasionally, for about 20 minutes until the vegetables are cooked thoroughly and are very soft, but not browned.

2 Meanwhile, rinse the vine leaves under cold, running water and pat dry with kitchen paper. Slice 4 thin slices off the lemon, then cut each slice in half. Finely grate the rind of half the lemon.

3 Stuff the mullet cavities with the lemon slices and remaining thyme sprigs. Rub a little olive oil on each fish and sprinkle with the lemon rind. Season with salt and pepper to taste.

4 Depending on the size of the mullet, wrap 5 or 6 vine leaves around each fish, to enclose it completely. Place the wrapped mullet on top of the fennel and peppers. Cover the pan and cook over a medium–low heat for 12–15 minutes until the fish are cooked through and the flesh flakes easily when it is tested with the tip of a knife.

5 Transfer the cooked fish to individual plates and spoon the fennel and peppers alongside. Garnish with thyme sprigs and serve.

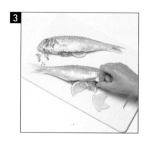

Plaice Fillets with Grapes

Fish is ideal for a quick meal, especially when cut into strips as in this recipe – it takes only minutes to cook.

NUTRITIONAL INFORMATION

Calories 226	Sugars 6g
Protein 23g	Fat 9g
Carbohydrate 9g	Saturates 4g

5 mins | 10 mins

SERVES 4

I N G R E D I E N T S

500 g/1 lb 2 oz plaice fillets, skinned

4 spring onions, white and green parts, sliced diagonally

125 ml/4 fl oz dry white wine

1 tbsp cornflour

2 tbsp skimmed milk

2 tbsp chopped fresh dill

4 tbsp double cream

125 g/4½ oz seedless white grapes

1 tsp lemon juice

salt and pepper

fresh dill sprigs, to garnish

TO SERVE

basmati rice

courgette ribbons

1 Cut the fish into short strips, about 4cm/ 1¾ inches long, and put these into a frying pan with the spring onions, white wine and seasoning.

2 Bring to the boil, cover and simmer for 4 minutes. Carefully transfer the fish to a warm serving dish. Cover and keep warm while you make the sauce.

3 Mix the cornflour and milk then add to the pan with the dill and cream. Bring to the boil, and boil, stirring, for 2 minutes until thickened.

4 Add the grapes and lemon juice and heat through gently for 1–2 minutes, then pour over the fish. Garnish with dill and serve with rice and courgette ribbons.

COOK'S TIP

Dill has a fairly strong aniseed flavour that goes very well with fish. The feathery leaves are particularly attractive when used as a garnish.

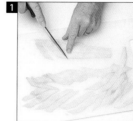

Potato-topped Cod

This simple dish has a spicy breadcrumb topping over layers of cod and potatoes. It is cooked in the oven until crisp and golden.

NUTRITIONAL INFORMATION

Calories	118	Sugars	.......1.0g
Protein	........9.8g	Fat	.........4.4g
Carbohydrate	..10.5g	Saturates	.....2.6g

5–10 mins   35 mins

SERVES 4

INGREDIENTS

5 tbsp butter

900 g/2 lb waxy potatoes, sliced

1 large onion, finely chopped

1 tsp wholegrain mustard

1 tsp garam masala

pinch of chilli powder

1 tbsp chopped fresh dill

75 g/2¾ oz fresh breadcrumbs

700 g/1 lb 9 oz cod fillet

50 g/1¾ oz Gruyère cheese, grated

salt and pepper

fresh dill sprigs, to garnish

1 Melt half of the butter in a frying pan. Add the potatoes and fry for 5 minutes, turning until they are browned all over. Remove the potatoes from the pan with a perforated spoon.

2 Add the remaining butter to the frying pan and stir in the onion, mustard, garam masala, chilli powder, dill and breadcrumbs. Cook for 1–2 minutes, stirring and mixing well.

3 Layer half of the potatoes in the base of an ovenproof dish and place the cod fillets on top. Cover the fillets with the rest of the potato slices. Season to taste.

4 Spoon the spicy mixture from the frying pan over the potato and sprinkle with the grated cheese.

5 Cook in a preheated oven, 200°C/400°F/Gas Mark 6, for 20–25 minutes or until the topping is golden and crisp and the fish is cooked through. Remove from the oven, garnish with fresh dill sprigs and serve at once.

COOK'S TIP

This dish is ideal served with baked vegetables, which can be cooked in the oven at the same time.

Warm Tuna Salad

A colourful, refreshing first course that is perfect to make for a special summer lunch or dinner. The dressing can be made in advance.

NUTRITIONAL INFORMATION

Calories . . . . .127 Sugars 4g
Protein . . . . .13g Fat 6g
Carbohydrate . . . .6g Saturates 1g

🍲 20 mins   🕐 10–15 mins

SERVES 4

I N G R E D I E N T S

50 g/1¾ oz Chinese leaves, shredded

3 tbsp rice wine

2 tbsp Thai fish sauce

1 tbsp fresh ginger root, finely shredded

1 garlic clove, finely chopped

½ small red bird's-eye chilli, finely chopped

2 tsp soft light brown sugar

2 tbsp lime juice

400 g/14 oz fresh tuna steak

sunflower oil for brushing

125 g/4½ oz cherry tomatoes

fresh mint leaves and mint sprigs, roughly chopped, to garnish

1 Place a small pile of shredded Chinese leaves on a serving plate. Place the rice wine, fish sauce, ginger, garlic, chilli, brown sugar and 1 tablespoon of the lime juice in a screw-top jar and shake well to combine ingredients.

2 Cut the tuna into strips of an even thickness. Sprinkle them with the remaining lime juice.

3 Brush a wide frying pan or griddle with the oil and heat until very hot. Arrange the tuna strips in the pan and cook until just firm and a light golden colour, turning them over once. Remove and set aside.

4 Add the tomatoes and cook over a high heat until lightly browned. Spoon the tuna and tomatoes over the Chinese leaves and pour on the dressing. Garnish with fresh mint and serve warm.

COOK'S TIP

You can make a quick version of this dish using canned tuna. Just drain and flake the tuna, omit steps 2 and 3 and continue as in the recipe.

Smoked Haddock Salad

Smoked haddock has an affinity with eggs. Here it is teamed
with hard-boiled quail's eggs and topped with a creamy chive dressing.

NUTRITIONAL INFORMATION

Calories 366	Sugars 3g	
Protein 26g	Fat 20g	
Carbohydrate ...21g	Saturates 5g	

15 mins   10 mins

SERVES 4

I N G R E D I E N T S

350 g/12 oz smoked haddock fillet

4 tbsp olive oil

1 tbsp lemon juice

2 tbsp soured cream

1 tbsp hot water

2 tbsp chopped fresh chives

1 plum tomato, peeled, deseeded and diced

8 quail's eggs

4 thick slices granary or multigrain bread

115 g/4 oz mixed salad leaves

chives, to garnish

salt and pepper

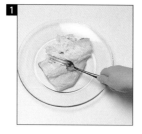  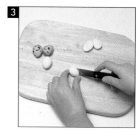

1 Fill a large frying pan with water and bring to the boil. Add the smoked haddock fillet, cover and remove from the heat. Leave for 10 minutes until the fish is tender. Lift from the poaching water, drain and leave until cool enough to handle. Flake the flesh, removing any small bones. Set aside. Discard the poaching water.

2 Whisk together the oil, lemon juice, soured cream, hot water, chives and seasoning. Stir in the tomato. Set aside.

3 Bring a small saucepan of water to the boil. Carefully lower the quail's

eggs into the water. Cook the eggs for 3–4 minutes from when the water returns to the boil (3 minutes for a slightly soft centre, 4 minutes for a firm centre). Drain immediately and refresh under cold running water. Carefully peel the eggs, cut in half lengthways and set aside.

4 Toast the granary bread and cut each slice across diagonally to form 4 triangles. Arrange 4 triangles on each of

4 serving plates. Top with the salad leaves, then the flaked fish and finally the quail's eggs. Spoon over the dressing and garnish with a few extra chives.

Lime- & Basil-cured Salmon

It is important to use fresh salmon for this dish. The salt and sugar draw the moisture from the fish, leaving it raw but cured and full of flavour.

NUTRITIONAL INFORMATION

Calories . . . . . . .382g Sugars 27g
Protein . . . . .31g Fat 17g
Carbohydrate . . .27g Saturates 3g

20 mins, plus refrigeration time

10 mins

SERVES 6

INGREDIENTS

900 g/2 lb very fresh salmon fillet, from the head end, skinned

50 g/1¾ oz sugar

50 g/1¾ oz sea salt

5 tbsp chopped fresh basil

finely grated rind of 2 limes

1 tsp white peppercorns, lightly crushed

DRESSING

200 ml/7 fl oz rice vinegar

5 tbsp sugar

finely grated rind of 1 lime

½ tsp English mustard

3 tbsp chopped fresh basil

1 tbsp Japanese pickled ginger, finely shredded

150 g/5½ oz mixed salad leaves, to serve

TO GARNISH

lime wedges

basil leaves

1 Remove any small pin bones that remain in the salmon fillet. Wash and dry the fish. Place the salmon in a large non-metallic dish and sprinkle evenly with the sugar, sea salt, basil, lime rind and peppercorns. Cover and chill for 24–48 hours, turning the fish occasionally.

2 For the dressing, put the rice vinegar and sugar in a small saucepan and stir gently over a low heat until the sugar has dissolved. Then, bring to the boil and simmer for 5–6 minutes until the liquid is reduced by about one-third. Remove the saucepan from the heat and stir in the lime rind and mustard. Put the saucepan to one side.

3 Remove the salmon fillet from the marinade, wiping off any excess with kitchen paper. Slice very thinly.

4 To serve, stir the chopped basil and ginger into the dressing. Toss the salad leaves with a little of the dressing and arrange on 6 serving plates. Divide the salmon slices between the plates and drizzle a little dressing over. Garnish with lime wedges and basil leaves.

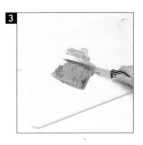

Caesar Salad

Caesar salad was the invention of a chef at a large hotel in Acapulco, Mexico. It has rightly earned an international reputation.

NUTRITIONAL INFORMATION

Calories 589	Sugars 3g	
Protein 11g	Fat 50g	
Carbohydrate ...24g	Saturates 9g	

30 mins   20 mins

SERVES 4

INGREDIENTS

1 large cos lettuce or
  2 hearts of romaine

4 anchovies, drained and
  halved lengthways

Parmesan shavings, to garnish

DRESSING

2 garlic cloves, crushed

1½ tsp Dijon mustard

1 tsp Worcestershire sauce

4 anchovies in olive oil, drained
  and chopped

1 egg yolk

1 tbsp lemon juice

150 ml/5 fl oz olive oil

4 tbsp freshly grated Parmesan cheese

salt and pepper

CROÛTONS

4 thick slices day-old bread

2 tbsp olive oil

1 garlic clove, crushed

1 Make the dressing. In a food processor or blender, put the garlic, mustard, Worcestershire sauce, anchovies, egg yolk, lemon juice and seasoning and blend together for 30 seconds, until foaming. Add the olive oil, drop by drop, until the mixture begins to thicken, then in a steady stream until all the oil is incorporated. Scrape out of the food processor or blender. Add a little hot water if the dressing is too thick. Stir in the grated Parmesan. Taste for seasoning and set aside in the refrigerator until required.

2 For the croûtons, cut the bread into 1-cm/½-inch cubes. Toss with the oil and garlic in a bowl. Transfer to a baking sheet in a single layer. Bake in a preheated oven at 180°C/350°F/ Gas Mark 4, for 15–20 minutes, stirring occasionally, until the croûtons are browned and crisp. Remove from the oven and allow to cool. Set aside.

3 Separate the lettuce into individual leaves and wash. Tear into pieces and spin dry in a salad spinner. Alternatively, dry the leaves on kitchen paper. Transfer to a plastic bag and refrigerate until needed.

4 Put the lettuce into a large serving bowl, add the dressing and toss until the leaves are coated. Top with halved anchovies, croûtons and Parmesan shavings. Serve at once while the croûtons are still hot.

Skate & Spinach Salad

This salad makes a filling main course. Fresh skate should have a faint smell of ammonia; if the smell is very strong, do not use the fish.

NUTRITIONAL INFORMATION

Calories . . . . .316 Sugars 18g
Protein . . . . .32g Fat 13g
Carbohydrate . . .18g Saturates 1g

15 mins   40 mins

SERVES 4

INGREDIENTS

700 g/1 lb 9 oz skate wings, trimmed

2 sprigs fresh rosemary

1 fresh bay leaf

1 tbsp black peppercorns

1 lemon, quartered

450 g/1 lb baby spinach leaves

1 tbsp olive oil

1 small red onion, thinly sliced

2 garlic cloves, crushed

½ tsp chilli flakes

50 g/1¾ oz pine kernels, lightly toasted

50 g/1¾ oz raisins

1 tbsp light muscovado sugar

2 tbsp chopped fresh parsley

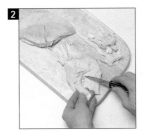

1 Put the skate wings into a large saucepan with the rosemary, bay leaf, peppercorns and lemon quarters. Cover with cold water and bring to the boil. Simmer, covered, for 4–5 minutes until the flesh begins to come away from the cartilage. Remove from the heat and leave for 15 minutes.

2 Lift the fish from the poaching water and remove the flesh by shredding it off. Set aside.

3 In a clean saucepan, cook the spinach (with just the water that clings to the leaves after washing) over a high heat for 30 seconds until just wilted. Drain, refresh under cold water and drain well once more. Squeeze out any excess water and set aside.

4 Heat the olive oil in a large, deep frying pan. Add the red onion and fry for 3–4 minutes until softened but not browned. Add the garlic, chilli flakes, pine kernels, raisins and sugar. Cook for 1–2 minutes, then add the spinach and toss for 1 minute until heated through.

5 Gently fold in the skate and cook for a further minute. Season well.

6 Divide the salad between 4 serving plates and sprinkle with the chopped parsley. Serve immediately.

Salpicon of Crab

This lightly spiced crab salad is a cooling treat for a hot day. Eat it with crisp tortilla chips, or wrapped in a warm corn tortilla.

NUTRITIONAL INFORMATION

Calories	186	Sugars	.........2g
Protein	........13g	Fat	...........13g
Carbohydrate	....3g	Saturates	.......2g

 20 mins   🕐 0 mins

SERVES 4

INGREDIENTS

¼ red onion, chopped

½–1 fresh green chilli, deseeded and chopped

juice of 1 lime

1 tbsp cider or other fruit vinegar, such as raspberry

1 tbsp chopped fresh coriander

1 tbsp extra-virgin olive oil

225–350 g/8–12 oz fresh crab meat

lettuce leaves, to serve

TO GARNISH

1 avocado

lime juice, for tossing

1–2 ripe tomatoes

3–5 radishes

VARIATION

For a toasted crab salad sandwich, split open a long roll or baguette and heap on crab salad. Top with a generous layer of cheese. Place the open roll under the grill to melt the cheese. Spread the toasted plain side with a little mayonnaise and close the sandwich up. Cut and serve with salsa.

1 Combine the onion with the chilli, lime juice, vinegar, fresh coriander and olive oil. Add the crab meat to the ingredients and toss lightly together.

2 To make the garnish, cut each avocado in half around the stone. Twist apart, then remove the stone with a knife. Carefully peel off the skin and slice the flesh. Toss the avocado gently in lime juice to prevent discoloration.

3 Halve the tomatoes, then remove the cores and seeds. Dice the flesh. Slice the radishes thinly.

4 Arrange the crab salad on a bed of lettuce leaves, garnish with the avocado, tomatoes and radishes and serve immediately.

Salade Niçoise

This classic salad from Nice is often made with canned tuna, but using seared fresh tuna steaks instead gives it a sophisticated twist.

NUTRITIONAL INFORMATION

Calories 356	Sugars 3g
Protein 22g	Fat 26g
Carbohydrate . . .10g	Saturates 4g

20 mins   25 mins

SERVES 4–6

INGREDIENTS

3 large eggs

250 g/9 oz French beans, topped and tailed

250 g/9 oz small waxy potatoes, such as Charlottes, scrubbed and halved

1 large, sun-ripened tomato, cut into eighths

1 large tuna steak, about 350 g/12 oz and 2 cm/¾ inch thick, seared (see page 66)

60 g/2 oz Provençal-style olives or plain black olives

50 g/1 ¾ oz canned anchovy fillets in oil, drained

1 tbsp chopped fresh flat-leaved parsley

GARLIC VINAIGRETTE

100 ml/3½ fl oz extra-virgin olive oil

3 tbsp red or white wine vinegar

½ tsp sugar

½ tsp Dijon mustard

2 garlic cloves, crushed

1 To make the vinaigrette, put all the ingredients in a screw-top jar and shake until blended. Season with salt and pepper to taste. Set aside.

2 Boil the eggs for 12 minutes. Drain them and then run under cold running water to stop them cooking further.

3 Put the beans and potatoes into separate pans of boiling water. Blanch the beans for 3 minutes, then drain and immediately transfer to a large bowl. Shake the dressing and pour it over the beans. Cook the potatoes until tender, then drain and add to the beans and dressing while still hot. Leave to cool.

4 Add the tomato, break the tuna into large chunks and gently toss with the other ingredients. Shell the eggs and then cut them into quarters.

5 Mound the tuna and vegetables on a large serving platter and surround with the eggs. Scatter with olives and a lattice of anchovies. Cover and chill.

6 About 15 minutes before serving, remove the salad from the refrigerator. Sprinkle with parsley and serve.

Lobster & Lime Salad

The lobster makes this a special-occasion salad, both in cost and flavour. The richness of the lobster meat is offset by the tangy lime dressing.

NUTRITIONAL INFORMATION

Calories 181	Sugars 0.8g	
Protein 6.8g	Fat 13.9g	
Carbohydrate ...7.6g	Saturates 2.2g	

🍳 5 mins   🕐 10–15 mins

SERVES 4

INGREDIENTS

450 g/1 lb waxy potatoes, scrubbed and sliced

225 g/8 oz cooked lobster meat

150 ml/5 fl oz mayonnaise

2 tbsp lime juice

finely grated rind of 1 lime

1 tbsp chopped fresh parsley

2 tbsp olive oil

2 tomatoes, deseeded and diced

2 hard-boiled eggs, quartered

1 tbsp quartered stoned green olives

salt and pepper

1 Cook the potatoes in a saucepan of boiling water for 10–15 minutes or until they are cooked through. Drain and reserve.

2 Remove the lobster meat from the shell and then separate it into large pieces.

3 In a bowl, mix together the mayonnaise, 1 tablespoon of the lime juice, half the grated lime rind and half the chopped parsley, then set aside.

4 In a separate bowl, whisk the remaining lime juice with the olive oil and pour the dressing over the potatoes. Arrange the potatoes on a serving plate.

5 Top with the lobster meat, tomatoes, eggs and olives. Season with salt and pepper to taste and sprinkle with the reserved parsley.

6 Spoon the mayonnaise on to the centre of the salad, top with the reserved rind and serve.

COOK'S TIP
As shellfish is used in this salad, serve it immediately, or keep covered and chilled for up to 1 hour before serving.

Sweet-&-Sour Fish Salad

This refreshing blend of pink and white fish mixed with fresh pineapple and peppers makes an interesting starter or a light meal.

NUTRITIONAL INFORMATION

Calories ....168 Sugars 5g
Protein ....24g Fat 6g
Carbohydrate ....5g Saturates 1g

35 mins   10 mins

SERVES 4

INGREDIENTS

225 g/8 oz trout fillets

225 g/8 oz white fish fillets (such as haddock or cod)

300 ml/10 fl oz water

1 stalk lemon grass

2 lime leaves

1 large red chilli

1 bunch spring onions, trimmed and shredded

115 g/4 oz fresh pineapple flesh, diced

1 small red pepper, deseeded and diced

1 bunch watercress, washed and trimmed

fresh snipped chives, to garnish

DRESSING

dressing

1 tbsp sunflower oil

1 tbsp rice wine vinegar

pinch of chilli powder

1 tsp clear honey

salt and pepper

1 Rinse the fish, place in a frying pan and pour over the water. Bend the lemon grass in half to bruise it and add to the pan with the lime leaves. Prick the chilli with a fork and add to the pan. Bring to the boil and simmer for 7–8 minutes. Leave to cool.

2 Drain the fish fillets thoroughly, then flake the flesh away from the skin with the tip of a knife and place it in a bowl. Gently stir in the spring onions, pineapple and red pepper.

3 Arrange the washed watercress on 4 serving plates and spoon the cooked fish mixture on top.

4 To make the sweet-and-sour dressing, mix all the ingredients together and season well. Spoon over the fish and serve garnished with chives.

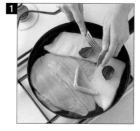

This is a Parragon Book
This edition published in 2003

Parragon
Queen Street House
4 Queen Street
Bath BA1 1HE, UK

ISBN: 1-40540-902-9

Printed in China

NOTE

This book uses metric and imperial measurements. Follow the same units
of measurement throughout; do not mix metric and imperial.
All spoon measurements are level: teaspoons are assumed to be 5 ml, and
tablespoons are assumed to be 15 ml. Unless otherwise stated,
milk is assumed to be full fat, eggs and individual vegetables such as potatoes
are medium, and pepper is freshly ground black pepper.

The nutritional information provided for each recipe is per serving or per person.
Optional ingredients, variations or serving suggestions have
not been included in the calculations. The times given for each recipe are an approximate
guide only because the preparation times may differ according to the techniques used by
different people and the cooking times may vary as a result of the type of oven used.

Recipes using raw or very lightly cooked eggs should be
avoided by infants, the elderly, pregnant women, convalescents,
and anyone suffering from an illness.

The publisher would like to thank
Steamer Trading Cookshop, Lewes, East Sussex, for the kind loan of props.

KS2
ARITHMETIC
SATs SUCCESS
TOPIC WORKBOOK

Ages 9–10

KS2
ARITHMETIC
SATs

TOPIC
WORKBOOK

PAUL BROADBENT

About this book

Mental arithmetic

Mental arithmetic involves carrying out calculations and working with numbers in your head, without the help of a calculator or computer. It is an important part of your child's education in maths and will help them to manage everyday situations in later life. This book will help your child to solve increasingly difficult problems in their head and at greater speed. It provides the opportunity to learn, practise and check progress in a wide range of mental arithmetic skills, such as addition, subtraction, multiplication, division and working with fractions, decimals and measures. This book will also aid preparation for the **Key Stage 2 mathematics** test.

Features of the book

Learn and revise – explains and refreshes mental arithmetic skills and strategies.

Practice activities – a variety of tasks to see how well your child has grasped each skill.

Mental arithmetic tests – 20 questions which test and reinforce your child's understanding of the preceding topics.

Speed tests and *Progress charts* – the one-minute tests challenge your child to carry out mental calculations at increasing speed and the progress charts enable them to record their results.

Key facts – a summary of key points that your child should learn by heart and memorise.

Answers are in a pull-out booklet at the centre of the book.

Mental arithmetic tips

- Cooking with your child provides opportunities to use measures – reading scales, converting between units and calculating with amounts.

- Look at prices and compare amounts when shopping. Use receipts to find differences between prices.

- Play board games, such as a simplified version of *Monopoly*, and dice games, such as *Yahtzee*, taking opportunities to add and subtract numbers and money.

- Addition and subtraction facts to 20 and the multiplication tables are basic key facts that your child will need to know so that they can solve problems with bigger numbers. Regularly practise these facts – you could write them on sticky notes around the house for your child to see or answer.

- Short, regular practice to build confidence is better than spending too long on an activity so that boredom creeps in. Keep each session to 20–30 minutes.

Contents

Counting and numbers   **4**

Place value   **6**

Ordering and rounding numbers   **8**

Mental arithmetic tests 1 and 2   **10–11**

Addition   **12**

Subtraction   **14**

Addition and subtraction problems   **16**

Mental arithmetic tests 3 and 4   **18–19**

Multiples, factors and primes   **20**

Multiplication   **22**

Division   **24**

Mental arithmetic tests 5 and 6   **26–27**

Fractions   **28**

Fractions of amounts   **30**

Fraction calculations   **32**

Mental arithmetic tests 7 and 8   **34–35**

Decimals   **36**

Fractions, decimals and percentages   **38**

Decimal calculations   **40**

Mental arithmetic tests 9 and 10   **42–43**

Square numbers   **44**

Area and perimeter   **46**

Time   **48**

Mental arithmetic tests 11 and 12   **50–51**

Speed tests and Progress charts   **52–57**

Key facts   **58**

Acknowledgements   **60**

Answers (centre pull-out)   **1–4**

Counting and numbers

Learn and revise

Look at the pattern in number sequences to continue them.

| 12 000 | 22 000 | 32 000 | 42 000 | _____ |

The next number is 52 000

You can also look at the difference between the numbers to work out the size of each step.

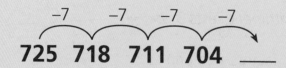

This is going down in sevens. The next number is 697.

When you count backwards past zero, you will use negative numbers. Picture them on a number line to help you see them in sequence.

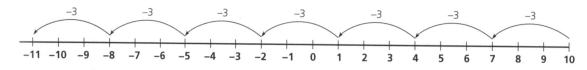

Practice activities

1. Write the missing numbers in each sequence.

    a) 108   158   _____   258   _____   358   _____

    b) _____   _____   6405   6505   6605   _____   6805

    c) 18   _____   4   −3   _____   _____   −24

    d) 7855   7825   7795   _____   _____   7705   _____

    e) −35   −20   _____   _____   _____   40   55

4

2. Two numbers in each sequence have been swapped over.
Circle the two numbers.

a) 480   478   468   474   472   470   476

b) 3165   3150   3155   3160   3145   3170   3175

c) 1144   1124   1136   1132   1128   1140   1120

3. This is the halfway number between 2016 and 2032.

2016 ------ 2024 ------ 2032

What are these halfway numbers?

a) 42 440 ------ _____ ------ 42 880

b) −34 --------- _____ ------ −6

c) 60 038 ------ _____ ------ 61 038

d) 91 458 ------ _____ ------ 95 458

4. Count in these steps. Write the missing numbers.

a) Count in 10s:

48 760   _____   _____   _____   48 800

b) Count in 10s:

−27   _____   _____   _____   13

c) Count in 100s:

20 845   _____   _____   _____   21 245

d) Count in 100s:

43 959   _____   _____   _____   44 359

e) Count in 1000s:

37 008   _____   _____   _____   41 008

f) Count in 1000s:

98 255   _____   _____   _____   102 255

Place value

Learn and revise

Look at this number and how it is made:

817 265 = 800 000 + 10 000 + 7000 + 200 + 60 + 5

eight hundred and seventeen thousand two hundred and sixty-five

Hundred thousands	Ten thousands	Thousands	Hundreds	Tens	Ones
8	1	7	2	6	5

800 000 > 10 000 > 7000 > 200 > 60 > 5 >

When you read large numbers, group the digits in threes starting with the ones digit. These are then easier to read:

340 285 ⟶ 340 *thousand* 285

Practice activities

1. Write the missing numbers.

   a) 72 195 = 70 000 + 2000 + _____ + _____ + _____

   b) 46 355 = _____ + _____ + _____ + 50 + 5

   c) 149 837 = 100 000 + _____ + _____ + _____ + 30 + _____

   d) 283 954 = _____ + _____ + _____ + _____ + _____ + 4

   e) 723 593 = _____ + 20 000 + _____ + _____ + _____ + _____

2. Write these as words.

   a) 23 456 _____

   _____

   b) 305 093 _____

   _____

3. Write down in words the value of the 2 digit in each number.

    a) 72 483   _____

    b) 248 660   _____

    c) 492 863   _____

    d) 820 357   _____

    e) 295 780   _____

    f) 372 009   _____

4. **a)** What number is 5000 more than 26 145?   _____

    b) What number is 10 000 more than 85 035?   _____

    c) What number is 50 000 less than 178 360?   _____

    d) What number is 20 000 less than 34 223?   _____

5. Write these numbers as figures.

    a) twenty-eight thousand two hundred and eight   _____

    b) four hundred and seven thousand two hundred   _____

    c) nine hundred thousand and six   _____

    d) six hundred and ninety thousand   _____

    e) one hundred and fifty-four thousand
       seven hundred and thirty-one   _____

    f) two hundred thousand and seventy-three   _____

6. Write the missing numbers for this multiplication machine.

IN	234		93		345
OUT		30 000		41 000	

Ordering and rounding numbers

Learn and revise

If you have a list of numbers to put in order, compare the place value of the digits in each number. Compare the largest value in each number and then the next largest, and so on.

Example: Put these in order, starting with the smallest.

189 456   17 432   190 355   18 045 $\longrightarrow$ 17 432   18 045   189 456   190 355

Rounding makes numbers easier to work with – change them to the nearest 10, 100, 1000 or 10 000. It is useful for estimating approximate answers.

Rounding 38 465 to the nearest:

    10 is 38 470
    100 is 38 500
    1000 is 38 000
    10 000 is 40 000

Practice activities

1. Write < or > to make these correct.

   a) 21 735 _____ 20 889

   b) 53 478 _____ 53 521

   c) 61 350 _____ 62 007

   d) 31 486 _____ 31 468

2. Underline the smallest number in this set. Draw a circle around the largest.

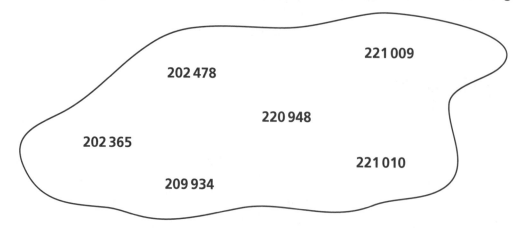

221 009

202 478

220 948

202 365

221 010

209 934

Ordering and rounding numbers

3. Write each set of numbers in order of size, starting with the smallest.

  a) 428 355   425 009   428 309   425 010

  _____   _____   _____   _____

  smallest

  b) 238 970   230 980   245 000   240 500

  _____   _____   _____   _____

  smallest

  c) 863 015   866 351   863 501   863 510

  _____   _____   _____   _____

  smallest

  d) 531 962   513 962   531 926   513 629

  _____   _____   _____   _____

  smallest

4. Round each of these numbers to the nearest 10.

  a) 6793   _____   **b)** 3586   _____

  c) 29 136   _____   **d)** 83 452   _____

  e) 276 834   _____   **f)** 579 356   _____

5. Round each of these numbers to the nearest 100.

  a) 2186   _____   **b)** 6754   _____

  c) 34 257   _____   **d)** 61 548   _____

  e) 843 956   _____   **f)** 286 541   _____

6. Round each of these numbers to the nearest 1000.

  a) 4845   _____   **b)** 7487   _____

  c) 36 404   _____   **d)** 43 529   _____

  e) 189 456   _____   **f)** 207 863   _____

Mental arithmetic test 1

1. Round each number to the nearest 10.

   58 834 $\longrightarrow$ _____

   927 015 $\longrightarrow$ _____

2. Write in words the value of the underlined digit.

   490 152

   _____

3. Multiply both numbers by 1000.

   26 _____

   519 _____

4. Circle the smallest number and underline the largest number.

   32 607   27 036   30 762

   26 703   32 076

5. Write the halfway number.

   −25   -------_____------- −5

6. Write the missing number.

   5195   5095   _____   4895   4795

7. Write two hundred and sixty-one thousand four hundred and ten as figures.

   _____

8. What number is 6000 less than 988 799?

   _____

9. Write the next number.

   44 372   44 272   44 172   _____

10. Make the smallest possible number from these digit cards.

    7   8   2
       1   3

    ⬠⬠⬠⬠⬠

11. What number is 30 000 more than 214 503?

    _____

12. Write < or > to make these correct.

    895 135 _____ 895 513 _____ 893 555

13. Count in 1000s. Write the missing numbers.

    58 820 _____ _____ 61 820

14. Write the missing numbers.

    −43   −23   _____   _____   37

15. Write in words the value of the underlined digit.

    5 706 289

    _____

16. Round each number to the nearest 1000.

    17 465 $\longrightarrow$ _____

    332 960 $\longrightarrow$ _____

17. Write in words the value of the underlined digit.

    917 264

    _____

18. Multiply both numbers by 100.

    2054 _____

    631 _____

19. Write < or > to make this correct.

    46 743 _____ 467 343

20. Write the next two numbers.

    18   10   2   _____   _____

Mental arithmetic test 2

1. Write in words the value of the underlined digit.

   970 480

   _____

2. Write < or > to make these correct.

   32 323 _____ 32 322

   675 707 _____ 767 507

3. What number is 2000 more than 541 045?

   _____

4. Make the largest possible number from these digit cards.

   [3] [7] [8]
     [0] [4] [1]

   ⬡⬡⬡⬡⬡⬡

5. Count in 10s and write the missing numbers.

   –23 _____ _____ _____ 17

6. Multiply both numbers by 1000.

   68 _____

   984 _____

7. Write the next two numbers.

   14   9   4   _____ _____

8. Write the missing number.

   1465   1515 _____ 1615

9. Round each number to the nearest 100.

   8544 ⟶ _____

   210 766 ⟶ _____

10. Write five hundred and twelve thousand six hundred and twenty as figures.

    _____

11. Round each number to the nearest 1000.

    91 837 ⟶ _____

    552 400 ⟶ _____

12. What number is 40 000 less than 578 899?

    _____

13. Write the next number.

    37 204   38 204   39 204 _____

14. Write four hundred and ninety-one thousand two hundred and six as figures.

    _____

15. Write the halfway number.

    74 140 ------- _____ ------- 78 140

16. Multiply both numbers by 100.

    525 _____

    1903 _____

17. Write < or > to make this correct.

    328 154 _____ 38 210

18. Write in words the value of the underlined digit.

    316 758

    _____

19. Write the missing numbers.

    –12 _____ –2   3 _____

20. Circle the smallest number and underline the largest number.

    814 950   815 049   809 451

    804 591   815 409

Score   /20

11

Addition

Learn and revise

Use any facts you know to help learn others.

$$8 + 6 = 14$$

You can use this to work out these and other facts:

$18 + 16 = 34$

$1800 + 1600 = 3400$

$4080 + 3060 = 7140$

$80 + 60 = 140$

$800 + 600 = 1400$

$5008 + 1006 = 6014$

Practice activities

1. Use the first answer to help with the others in each set.

   a) $7 + 6$ = _____

   $70 + 60$ = _____ $700 + 600$ = _____

   $1007 + 3006$ = _____ $2070 + 4060$ = _____

   b) $9 + 5$ = _____

   $90 + 50$ = _____ $900 + 500$ = _____

   $49 + 25$ = _____ $1090 + 6050$ = _____

   c) $3 + 8$ = _____

   $30 + 80$ = _____ $300 + 800$ = _____

   $6300 + 2800$ = _____ $4030 + 3080$ = _____

   d) $8 + 7$ = _____

   $80 + 70$ = _____ $800 + 700$ = _____

   $58 + 37$ = _____ $3080 + 2070$ = _____

2. Write the missing numbers on these addition walls. Each missing number is the sum of the two numbers below.

a)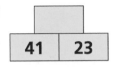
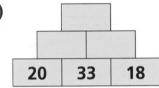

41 | 23

b)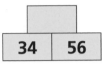

34 | 56

c)
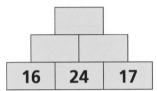

39 | 42

d)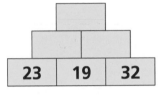

20 | 33 | 18

e)

23 | 19 | 32

f)

16 | 24 | 17

3. Look at these numbers and answer the questions.

1405   2002   2404   3003

a) Add together the two odd numbers. _____

b) What is the total of the two smallest numbers? _____

c) Add together the two even numbers. _____

d) What is the total of the two largest numbers? _____

e) Find the total of the three largest numbers. _____

4. Look at these.

1234 + 8765 = 9999   **3333 + 6666 = 9999**

Find four more 4-digit additions that total 9999.

_____ + _____ = 9999

_____ + _____ = 9999

_____ + _____ = 9999

_____ + _____ = 9999

Subtraction

Learn and revise

There are different strategies you can use to subtract mentally.

Counting on from the smallest number is a good method.

Example: What is 320 subtract 170?

Count on from 170 to
200 and then to 320.

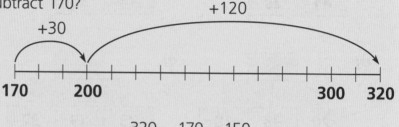

$$320 - 170 = 150$$

You could try breaking numbers up so that you can subtract them in your head.

Example: Take away 150 from 192.

$$192 - 150 =$$

$$190 + 2 - 150 =$$

$$190 - 150 + 2 = 40 + 2 = 42$$

Practice activities

1. Use the number lines to help you subtract these mentally.

a)
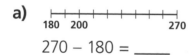

$$270 - 180 = \underline{\hspace{1cm}}$$

b)

240   300   410

$$410 - 240 = \underline{\hspace{1cm}}$$

c)

180   200   300   325

$$325 - 180 = \underline{\hspace{1cm}}$$

d)

250   300   345

$$345 - 250 = \underline{\hspace{1cm}}$$

e)

270   300   400   455

$$455 - 270 = \underline{\hspace{1cm}}$$

2. Answer these.

a) Take 35 away from 92. _____

b) Subtract 130 from 208. _____

c) What is 49 less than 120? _____

d) Take away 63 from 101. _____

e) What is 121 take away 97? _____

3. Look at these numbers and answer the questions.

1200   **3100**   **2800**   **3900**

a) Which two numbers have a difference of 300?

_____ and _____

b) Which number is 100 less than 4000?

_____

c) Which two numbers have a difference of 1600?

_____ and _____

4. Complete each chart to show the numbers coming out of each subtraction machine.

a)

IN	330	500	410	365	315	405
OUT	90					

b)

IN	570	640	410	500	730	620
OUT						

Addition and subtraction problems

Learn and revise

Look out for addition and subtraction words in any problems. They can give a clue for how to solve the problem.

Addition words	Subtraction words
add, total, altogether, sum, plus, more than, increase	subtract, take away, minus, less than, fewer, difference, reduce

Be careful though, some problems are confusing. Read them carefully and 'picture' the problem.

Practice activities

1. Answer these to find out how much is left for each one.

   a) A jug holds 1200 ml of orange juice. 750 ml is poured into one glass and 350 ml into another glass.

   How much orange juice is left? _____ ml

   b) Megan buys 5500 mm of cloth. She cuts off a piece 1400 mm long to make a skirt and cuts another piece of 2500 mm to make a scarf.

   How much cloth is left over? _____ mm

   c) Mrs Wise buys a 3200 g box of washing powder. She gives 1800 g to her sister and uses 900 g herself.

   How much washing powder is left in the box? _____ g

   e) A farmer collects 370 eggs one week and 420 the next week. He has to throw 35 away as they were cracked.

   How many eggs does he have left to take to market? _____

Addition and subtraction problems

2. Two boxes of paper have a difference in weight of 3600 g. When they are put together, they have a total weight of 6400 g. What is the weight of each box of paper?

_____ g and _____ g

3. These are the lengths of some of the longest rivers in the world, rounded to the nearest 10 km. Answer the questions that follow.

River	Continent	Length
Nile	Africa	6690 km
Amazon	S. America	6380 km
Mississippi	N. America	6270 km
Chang Jiang	Asia	6210 km

a) What is the difference in length between the two longest rivers in the world, the Nile and the Amazon?

_____ km

b) Which river is 480 km shorter than the Nile? _____

c) Which two rivers have a difference in length of 420 km?

_____

4. A school is collecting bottle tops for recycling. It is aiming for a target of 3000 bottle tops. These are the totals for the first three months:

Month	Bottle tops collected
January	800
February	690
March	710

How many more bottle tops does the school need to collect to reach its target?

_____

Mental arithmetic test 3

1. 320 − 280 = _____

2. Answer these.

   40 + 70 = _____

   3400 + 2700 = _____

3. A school has 560 children. 285 are girls. How many boys are there?

   _____

4. What is 100 less than 6000?

   _____

5. What is the total of 1490 and 6204?

   _____

6. Take 45 away from 80. _____

7. Two parcels weigh 2800 g and 1300 g. What is the total weight of the parcels?

   _____ g

8. 56 + 28 = _____

   These are the amounts of water used by one person in one year. Use these amounts to answer 9–10.

   Daily normal shower = 2200 litres

   Daily power shower = 8030 litres

9. How much less water is used over a year using a normal shower than a power shower?

   _____ litres

10. How much water would two people use over a year if they had a normal shower every day?

    _____ litres

11. Circle the odd one out.

    6473 + 1304   5281 + 3607

          2764 + 5013   4025 + 3752

12. What is 108 take away 94?

    _____

13. 415 − 350 = _____

14. 3008 + 2005 = _____

15. 1450 ml of milk is used from a 2500 ml jug. How much milk is left in the jug?

    _____ ml

16. Add together 2003, 5406 and 1401.

    _____

17. Circle two numbers that have a difference of 1500.

              6500   7200

       5700   6200   5100

18. 430 − 280 = _____

19. 27 + 43 = _____

20. A train travels 635 km from London to Edinburgh. How far is the return journey there and back again?

    _____ km

Score   /20

1. 37 + 39 = _____

2. Circle two numbers that have a difference of 400.

   3200   3900

4100   3700   4200

3. 440 − 170 = _____

4. Circle the odd one out.

4725 + 4163   1208 + 7680

   3561 + 5217   2353 + 6535

5. Two of the highest mountains in Britain are Ben Nevis at 1344 m and Snowdon at 1085 m. How much higher is Ben Nevis than Snowdon?

_____ m

6. Take 32 away from 100. _____

7. 305 − 203 = _____

8. Answer these.

   90 + 20 = _____

5900 + 2200 = _____

Look at these numbers for 9–10.

   3501   1500   2425   4030

9. What is the difference between the largest and the smallest number?

_____

10. What is the total of the two odd numbers?

_____

11. 4060 + 3060 = _____

12. Subtract 76 from 110. _____

13. There are 350 pages in a book. Sam read 75 pages at school and another 60 pages at home. How many more pages are left for Sam to read?

_____

14. 45 + 35 = _____

15. A cake is made with 350 g flour, 175 g butter and 140 g sugar. What is the total weight of the cake?

_____ g

16. Add together 2380 and 5107.

_____

17. What is 10 less than 2000?

_____

18. It is 1460 m from Jo's house to school. She walks to school and back home every day. How far in total does she walk each day?

_____ m

19. 625 − 250 = _____

20. What is the total of these three numbers?

2303   5005   1605

_____

Score   /20

Multiples, factors and primes

Learn and revise

A **multiple** of a whole number is produced by multiplying that number by another whole number.

Multiples of 3 ⟶	3	6	9	12	15	18...	60...	300...
	×1	×2	×3	×4	×5	×6...	×20...	×100...
Multiples of 4 ⟶	4	8	12	16	20	24...	80...	400...

12 is a multiple of both 3 and 4.

This means that 12 is a **common multiple** of 3 and 4.

Factors of a number can divide that number exactly.

Factors of 18:

18 = 1 × 18   18 = 2 × 9   18 = 3 × 6

In order: 1, 2, 3, 6, 9, 18

In pairs: (1, 18), (2, 9), (3, 6)

A **prime number** has only two factors: 1 and itself.

2, 3, 5, 7 and 11 are the first five prime numbers.

Practice activities

1. Write the numbers in the correct part of this Venn diagram.

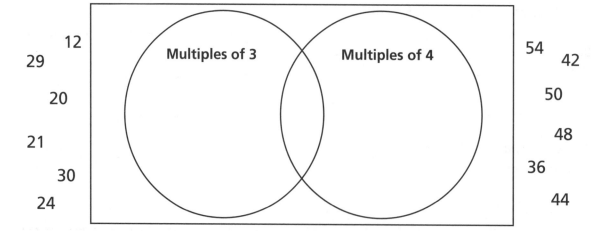

Multiples, factors and primes

2. Circle the correct answer for each of these.

a) A common multiple of 3 and 5 is:

35   45   55

b) A common multiple of 2 and 3 is:

28   38   48

c) A common multiple of 5 and 6 is:

70   80   90

d) A common multiple of 3 and 10 is:

100   120   160

3. Write the factors of these numbers in pairs.

a) 27 _____

b) 60 _____

c) 42 _____

d) 48 _____

4. Use these numbers to answer each question.

| 12 | 8 |
| 9 | 5 |

a) Which number is a factor of 64? ____

b) Which number is a factor of 35? ____

c) Which two numbers are factors of 36? ____ and ____

d) Which two numbers are factors of 60? ____ and ____

5. Find the factors of these prime numbers and square numbers.

a) Write the factors for each number in order.

Prime numbers

19 _____

23 _____

5 _____

37 _____

Square numbers

16 _____

9 _____

25 _____

36 _____

b) What do you notice about the number of factors for prime numbers?

_____

c) What do you notice about the number of factors for square numbers?

_____

Multiplication

Learn and revise

Use the tables facts that you know to help you multiply bigger numbers.

$$8 \times 4 = 32$$
$$80 \times 40 = 3200$$

Partition numbers and mentally calculate each part to make them easier to work with.

Follow these steps to answer 83 multiplied by 4:

83×4 is the same as 80×4 added to 3×4

$320 + 12 = 332$

So $83 \times 4 = 332$

Practice activities

1. Answer these.

   a) $7 \times 9 \quad =$ ____

   $70 \times 90 =$ _____

   b) $6 \times 3 \quad =$ ____

   $60 \times 30 \quad =$ _____

   c) $8 \times 6 \quad =$ ____

   $80 \times 60 =$ _____

   d) $9 \times 9 \quad =$ ____

   $90 \times 90 \quad =$ _____

   e) $7 \times 8 \quad =$ ____

   $70 \times 80 =$ _____

   f) $9 \times 12 \quad =$ ____

   $90 \times 120 =$ _____

2. Complete this multiplication grid.

×	32	54	45
6			
3			
8			

3. Answer these.

    a) 46 × 3 = _____   **b)** 39 × 5 = _____   **c)** 28 × 6 = _____

    d) 54 × 4 = _____   **e)** 81 × 3 = _____   **f)** 65 × 8 = _____

4. Multiply these sets of three numbers.

  a) 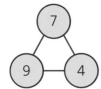   **b)**   **c)** 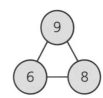   **d)**

    _____   _____   _____   _____

5. Use these digits.

    5   **6**   **9**

Arrange the three digits to make multiplications like this:

    9 **6** × **5** =

a) Arrange the digits to make the largest product.

    ☐☐ × ☐ = ___

b) Arrange the digits to make the smallest product.

    ☐☐ × ☐ = ___

c) Arrange the digits to make the product as close as possible to 500.

    ☐☐ × ☐ = ___

Division

Break numbers up to help you work out division answers.

Example: What is 94 divided by 4?

Break 94 up into 80 and 14.

$$80 \div 4 = 20$$
$$14 \div 4 = 3 \text{ r } 2$$
$$\text{So } 94 \div 4 = 23 \text{ r } 2$$

When there is a remainder it can be represented in different ways.

$94 \div 4 = 23 \text{ r } 2$ or... $94 \div 4 = 23\frac{1}{2}$ or... $94 \div 4 = 23.5$

Practice activities

1. Write the missing numbers. Use your multiplication and division facts to help you answer each one.

    a) $27 \div \boxed{} = 3$

    b) $28 \div 4 = \boxed{}$

    c) $\boxed{} \div 9 = 4$

    d) $24 \div 8 = \boxed{}$

    e) $49 \div \boxed{} = 7$

    f) $\boxed{} \div 3 = 6$

    g) $27 \div 9 = \boxed{}$

    h) $54 \div \boxed{} = 6$

    i) $56 \div 7 = \boxed{}$

    j) $\boxed{} \div 12 = 8$

    k) $110 \div 11 = \boxed{}$

    l) $\boxed{} \div 6 = 12$

2. Answer these.

a) 96 ÷ 4 = _____

b) 105 ÷ 5 = _____

c) 93 ÷ 3 = _____

d) 84 ÷ 6 = _____

e) 112 ÷ 7 = _____

f) 112 ÷ 4 = _____

g) 126 ÷ 6 = _____

h) 153 ÷ 3 = _____

3. Answer these and show the remainders in three different ways.

a) 47 ÷ 4 = _____ or _____ or _____

b) 83 ÷ 5 = _____ or _____ or _____

c) 91 ÷ 2 = _____ or _____ or _____

d) 97 ÷ 10 = _____ or _____ or _____

e) 69 ÷ 4 = _____ or _____ or _____

f) 99 ÷ 5 = _____ or _____ or _____

4. Complete each chart with the numbers coming out of each division machine.

a)

IN	1100	3300	7700	9900	11 000	13 200
OUT	100					

b)

IN	4800	2400	6000	9600	12 000	14 400
OUT						

Mental arithmetic test 5

1. What is the next prime number after 13?

_____

2. $49 \div 7 =$ _____

3. Write the missing pair of factors for 18.

(1, 18) (2, 9) (_____, _____)

4. Answer these.

$9 \times 6 =$ _____

$90 \times 60 =$ _____

5. $28 \times 5 =$ _____

6. Answer this, writing the remainder as a decimal.

$55 \div 2 =$ _____

7. $8800 \div 11 =$ _____

8. Circle the number that is **not** a prime number.

21   41

11   31

9. Write the missing factor for 16.

1, 2, _____ , 8, 16

10. $40 \times 70 =$ _____

11. Circle the number that is a common multiple of 5 and 3.

40

70   60

12. $36 \div 12 =$ _____

13. $53 \times 7 =$ _____

14. What is the remainder when 58 is divided by 6?

r = _____

15. Write < or > to make this correct.

8×24 _____ 2×84

16. Multiply these three numbers.

8 **3** **5**

_____

17. Answer this, writing the remainder as a fraction.

$72 \div 5 =$ _____

Look at these numbers for 18–20.

4   **8**   **5**   **12**

18. Which number is a multiple of 3? _____

19. Which number is **not** a factor of 60?

_____

20. Which number is a factor of 52? _____

Score   /20

26

Mental arithmetic test 6

1. 55 ÷ 11 = _____

2. Answer these.

    8 × 9 = _____

    80 × 90 = _____

3. What is the remainder when 45 is divided by 6?

    r = _____

4. Circle the number that is a common multiple of 2 and 4.

    28

    18   38

5. 56 ÷ 8 = _____

6. 37 × 5 = _____

7. Multiply these three numbers.

    _____

8. 80 × 30 = _____

9. Answer this, writing the remainder as a fraction.

    93 ÷ 10 = _____

10. Write the missing pair of factors for 30.

    (1, 30) (2, 15) (3, 10) (_____, _____)

11. What is the next prime number after 19?

    _____

12. Answer this, writing the remainder as a decimal.

    50 ÷ 4 = _____

13. 63 × 7 = _____

14. Write < or > to make this correct.

    9 × 34 _____ 4 × 93

15. 24 ÷ 12 = _____

16. Write the missing factor for 36.

    1, 2, 3, 4, _____, 9, 12, 18, 36

17. Circle the number that is **not** a prime number.

                23   43

        13   33

    Look at these numbers for 18–20.

        12   9   6   7

18. Which number is a multiple of 4? _____

19. Which number is **not** a factor of 36?

    _____

20. Which number is a factor of 45?

    _____

Fractions

Learn and revise

Proper fractions

If the numerator is smaller than the denominator, it is known as a **proper fraction**. The value of each fraction is less than 1, e.g.

$$\frac{1}{6} \qquad \frac{3}{4} \qquad \frac{7}{10}$$

Improper fractions

If the numerator is larger than the denominator, it is known as an **improper fraction**. The value of each fraction is greater than 1, e.g.

$$\frac{3}{2} \qquad \frac{7}{4} \qquad \frac{10}{7}$$

This shows seven slices of melon. Each slice is $\frac{1}{4}$ of a whole melon.

There is one whole melon and $\frac{3}{4}$ of a melon.

$\frac{4}{4} + \frac{3}{4} = \frac{7}{4}$ or $1\frac{3}{4}$

$\frac{7}{4}$ is an improper fraction. $1\frac{3}{4}$ is a mixed number.

Practice activities

1. Write these as mixed numbers and improper fractions.

a)

Mixed number: _____

Improper fraction: _____

b)

Mixed number: _____

Improper fraction: _____

c)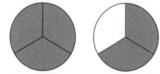

Mixed number: _____

Improper fraction: _____

d)

Mixed number: _____

Improper fraction: _____

2. Change these mixed numbers to improper fractions.

a) $2\frac{1}{4}$ = _____

b) $4\frac{1}{3}$ = _____

c) $1\frac{5}{8}$ = _____

d) $3\frac{3}{4}$ = _____

e) $2\frac{2}{5}$ = _____

f) $1\frac{1}{6}$ = _____

3. Change these improper fractions to mixed numbers.

a) $\frac{3}{2}$ = _____

b) $\frac{5}{4}$ = _____

c) $\frac{10}{3}$ = _____

d) $\frac{8}{7}$ = _____

e) $\frac{15}{2}$ = _____

f) $\frac{16}{3}$ = _____

4. Write the fraction each arrow points to, as a mixed number and an improper fraction.

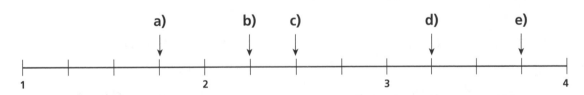

a) = _____ or _____

b) = _____ or _____

c) = _____ or _____

d) = _____ or _____

e) = _____ or _____

5. Write these in order, starting with the smallest.

$\frac{14}{4}$ $\qquad$ $3\frac{3}{4}$ $\qquad$ $\frac{12}{4}$ $\qquad$ $2\frac{1}{4}$ $\qquad$ $4\frac{1}{2}$ $\qquad$ $\frac{11}{2}$

_____ _____ _____ _____ _____ _____

smallest

Fractions of amounts

Learn and revise

Here are 20 oranges.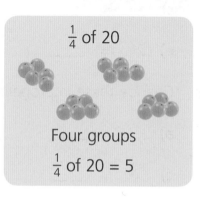

Which would give you the greatest number of oranges?

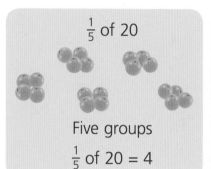 $\frac{1}{5}$ of 20

Five groups

$\frac{1}{5}$ of 20 = 4

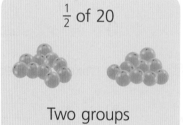 $\frac{1}{2}$ of 20

Two groups

$\frac{1}{2}$ of 20 = 10

$\frac{1}{4}$ of 20

Four groups

$\frac{1}{4}$ of 20 = 5

$\frac{1}{2}$ is greater than $\frac{1}{4}$ and $\frac{1}{4}$ is greater than $\frac{1}{5}$. $\frac{1}{2} > \frac{1}{4} > \frac{1}{5}$

Practice activities

1. Circle the fraction that gives the largest amount. Use the pictures to help.

    a) 18 balls

    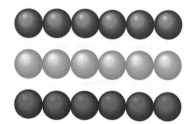

    $\frac{1}{6}$ $\frac{1}{3}$

    b) 16 balls

    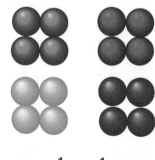

    $\frac{1}{4}$ $\frac{1}{2}$

    c) 21 balls

    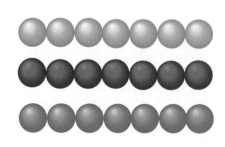

    $\frac{1}{3}$ $\frac{1}{7}$

    d) 18 balls

    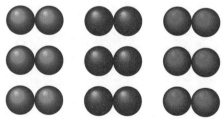

    $\frac{1}{6}$ $\frac{1}{9}$

Answers

Pages 4–5
1. a) 208, 308, 408   b) 6205, 6305, 6705
    c) 11, –10, –17   d) 7765, 7735, 7675
    e) –5, 10, 25
2. a) 468, 476   b) 3165, 3145   c) 1124, 1140
3. a) 42660   b) –20   c) 60538   d) 93458
4. a) 48770, 48780, 48790   b) –17, –7, 3
    c) 20945, 21045, 21145   d) 44059, 44159, 44259
    e) 38008, 39008, 40008   f) 99255, 100255, 101255

Pages 6–7
1. a) 100, 90, 5
    b) 40000, 6000, 300
    c) 40000, 9000, 800, 7
    d) 200000, 80000, 3000, 900, 50
    e) 700000, 3000, 500, 90, 3
2. a) twenty-three thousand four hundred and fifty-six
    b) three hundred and five thousand and ninety-three
3. a) two thousand   b) two hundred thousand
    c) two thousand   d) twenty thousand
    e) two hundred thousand   f) two thousand
4. a) 31145   b) 95035   c) 128360   d) 14223
5. a) 28208   b) 407200   c) 900006
    d) 690000   e) 154731   f) 200073
6. Top row should be completed as follows: 30, 41
    Bottom row should be completed as follows:
    234000, 93000, 345000

Pages 8–9
1. a) >   b) <   c) <   d) >
2. 202365, (221010)
3. a) 425009, 425010, 428309, 428355
    b) 230980, 238970, 240500, 245000
    c) 863015, 863501, 863510, 866351
    d) 513629, 513962, 531926, 531962
4. a) 6790   b) 3590   c) 29140
    d) 83450   e) 276830   f) 579360
5. a) 2200   b) 6800   c) 34300
    d) 61500   e) 844000   f) 286500
6. a) 5000   b) 7000   c) 36000
    d) 44000   e) 189000   f) 208000

Page 10
1. 58830, 927020   2. four hundred thousand
3. 26000, 519000   4. (26703) 32607
5. –15   6. 4995
7. 261410   8. 982799
9. 44072   10. 12378
11. 244503   12. <, >
13. 59820, 60820   14. –3, 17
15. seven hundred thousand   16. 17000, 333000
17. seven thousand   18. 205400, 63100
19. <   20. –6, –14

Page 11
1. nine hundred thousand   2. >, <
3. 543045   4. 874310
5. –13, –3, 7   6. 68000, 984000
7. –1, –6   8. 1565
9. 8500, 210800   10. 512620
11. 92000, 552000   12. 538899
13. 40204   14. 491206
15. 76140   16. 52500, 190300
17. >   18. six thousand
19. –7, 8   20. (804591) 815409

Pages 12–13
1. a) 13, 130, 1300, 4013, 6130
    b) 14, 140, 1400, 74, 7140
    c) 11, 110, 1100, 9100, 7110
    d) 15, 150, 1500, 95, 5150

2. a) 64   b) 90   c) 81   d) 104, 53, 51
    e) 93, 42, 51   f) 81, 40, 41
3. a) 4408   b) 3407   c) 4406   d) 5407
    e) 7409
4. There are many possible answers. Check all additions
    total 9999.

Pages 14–15
1. a) 90   b) 170   c) 145   d) 95   e) 185
2. a) 57   b) 78   c) 71   d) 38   e) 24
3. a) 3100 and 2800   b) 3900   c) 1200 and 2800
4. a) Bottom row should be completed as follows:
       260, 170, 125, 75, 165
    b) Bottom row should be completed as follows:
       190, 260, 30, 120, 350, 240

Pages 16–17
1. a) 100ml   b) 1600mm   c) 500g   d) 755
2. 1400g and 5000g
3. a) 310km   b) Chang Jiang
    c) Nile and Mississippi
4. 800

Page 18
1. 40   2. 110, 6100
3. 275   4. 5900
5. 7694   6. 35
7. 4100g   8. 84
9. 5830litres   10. 4400 litres
11. 5281 + 3607   12. 14
13. 65   14. 5013
15. 1050ml   16. 8810
17. 5700 and 7200   18. 150
19. 70   20. 1270km

Page 19
1. 76   2. 3700 and 4100
3. 270   4. 3561 + 5217
5. 259m   6. 68
7. 102   8. 110, 8100
9. 2530   10. 5926
11. 7120   12. 34
13. 215   14. 80
15. 665g   16. 7487
17. 1990   18. 2920m
19. 375   20. 8913

Pages 20–21
1.

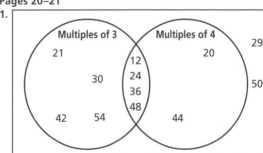

2. a) 45   b) 48   c) 90   d) 120
3. a) (1, 27) (3, 9)
    b) (1, 60) (2, 30) (3, 20) (4, 15) (5, 12) (6, 10)
    c) (1, 42) (2, 21) (3, 14) (6, 7)
    d) (1, 48) (2, 24) (3, 16) (4, 12) (6, 8)
4. a) 8   b) 5   c) 12, 9   d) 12, 5
5. a) **Prime numbers:**
       19 → 1, 19; 23 → 1, 23;
       5 → 1, 5; 37 → 1, 37
       Square numbers:
       16 → 1, 2, 4, 8, 16
       9 → 1, 3, 9

Answers

$25 \rightarrow 1, 5, 25$
$36 \rightarrow 1, 2, 3, 4, 6, 9, 12, 18, 36$
b) There are only two factors.
c) There are an odd number of factors.

Pages 22–23
1. **a)** 63, 6300 **b)** 18, 1800 **c)** 48, 4800
   d) 81, 8100 **e)** 56, 5600 **f)** 108, 10800
2.

×	32	54	45
6	192	324	270
3	96	162	135
8	256	432	360

3. **a)** 138 **b)** 195 **c)** 168 **d)** 216
   e) 243 **f)** 520
4. **a)** 252 **b)** 240 **c)** 432 **d)** 168
5. **a)** $65 \times 9 = 585$ **b)** $69 \times 5 = 345$ **c)** $56 \times 9 = 504$

Pages 24–25
1. **a)** 9 **b)** 7 **c)** 36 **d)** 3 **e)** 7 **f)** 18
   g) 3 **h)** 9 **i)** 8 **j)** 96 **k)** 10 **l)** 72
2. **a)** 24 **b)** 21 **c)** 31 **d)** 14 **e)** 16
   f) 28 **g)** 21 **h)** 51
3. **a)** 11 r 3 or $11\frac{3}{4}$ or 11.75 **b)** 16 r 3 or $16\frac{3}{5}$ or 16.6
   c) 45 r 1 or $45\frac{1}{2}$ or 45.5 **d)** 9 r 7 or $9\frac{7}{10}$ or 9.7
   e) 17 r 1 or $17\frac{1}{4}$ or 17.25 **f)** 19 r 4 or $19\frac{4}{5}$ or 19.8
4. **a)** Bottom row should be completed as follows:
      300, 700, 900, 1000, 1200
   b) Bottom row should be completed as follows:
      400, 200, 500, 800, 1000, 1200

Page 26
1. 17 **2.** 7 **3.** (3, 6) **4.** 54, 5400
5. 140 **6.** 27.5 **7.** 800 **8.** 21
9. 4 **10.** 2800 **11.** 60 **12.** 3
13. 371 **14.** 4 **15.** > **16.** 120
17. $14\frac{2}{5}$ **18.** 12 **19.** 8 **20.** 4

Page 27
1. 5 **2.** 72, 7200 **3.** 3 **4.** 28
5. 7 **6.** 185 **7.** 168 **8.** 2400
9. $9\frac{3}{10}$ **10.** (5, 6) **11.** 23 **12.** 12.5
13. 441 **14.** < **15.** 2 **16.** 6
17. 33 **18.** 12 **19.** 7 **20.** 9

Pages 28–29
1. **a)** $1\frac{2}{3}, \frac{5}{3}$ **b)** $3\frac{1}{2}, \frac{7}{2}$ **c)** $2\frac{2}{5}, \frac{12}{5}$ **d)** $2\frac{1}{6}, \frac{13}{6}$
2. **a)** $\frac{9}{4}$ **b)** $\frac{13}{3}$ **c)** $\frac{13}{8}$ **d)** $\frac{15}{4}$
   e) $\frac{12}{5}$ **f)** $\frac{7}{6}$
3. **a)** $1\frac{1}{2}$ **b)** $1\frac{1}{4}$ **c)** $3\frac{1}{3}$ **d)** $1\frac{1}{7}$
   e) $7\frac{1}{2}$ **f)** $5\frac{1}{3}$
4. **a)** $1\frac{3}{4}, \frac{7}{4}$ **b)** $2\frac{1}{4}, \frac{9}{4}$ **c)** $2\frac{1}{2}, \frac{5}{2}$ **d)** $3\frac{1}{4}, \frac{13}{4}$
   e) $3\frac{3}{4}, \frac{15}{4}$
5. $2\frac{1}{4}, \frac{12}{4}, \frac{14}{4}, 3\frac{3}{4}, 4\frac{1}{2}, \frac{11}{2}$

Pages 30–31
1. **a)** $\frac{1}{3}$ **b)** $\frac{1}{2}$
   c) $\frac{1}{3}$ **d)** $\frac{1}{6}$
2. **a)** < **b)** <
   c) > **d)** <
3. **a)** $\frac{1}{2}, \frac{1}{5}, \frac{1}{10}, \frac{1}{4}, \frac{3}{4}$ **b)** $\frac{1}{10}, \frac{1}{2}, \frac{1}{4}, \frac{3}{4}, \frac{1}{5}$
   c) $\frac{1}{4}, \frac{1}{2}, \frac{1}{10}, \frac{3}{4}, \frac{1}{5}$
4. **a)** $\frac{1}{10}$ of 10 kg **b)** thirds
   c) more time sleeping **d)** more spotted fish

Pages 32–33
1. $1\frac{3}{4} \rightarrow 1\frac{1}{4}$ $2\frac{3}{10} \rightarrow \frac{7}{10}$ $1\frac{7}{8} \rightarrow 1\frac{1}{8}$
   $2\frac{1}{3} \rightarrow \frac{2}{3}$ $1\frac{1}{3} \rightarrow 1\frac{1}{3}$

2. **a)** $\frac{8}{4}$ (or 2) **b)** $\frac{6}{10}$ (or $\frac{3}{5}$) **c)** $\frac{9}{5}$ (or $1\frac{4}{5}$) **d)** $\frac{8}{10}$ (or $\frac{4}{5}$)
3. **a)** $\frac{6}{4}$ or $1\frac{1}{2}$ **b)** $\frac{7}{6}$ or $1\frac{1}{6}$ **c)** $\frac{11}{10}$ or $1\frac{1}{10}$ **d)** $\frac{6}{5}$ or $1\frac{1}{5}$
4. **a)** $\frac{1}{2}$ or $\frac{2}{4}$ **b)** $\frac{3}{5}$ **c)** $\frac{7}{10}$ **d)** $\frac{2}{3}$
5. **a)** 7 **b)** $\frac{6}{10}$ m (or $\frac{3}{5}$ m) **c)** $6\frac{1}{5}$ **d)** $2\frac{3}{10}$ litres
   e) $8\frac{1}{2}$ (or $8\frac{4}{4}$)

Page 34
1. 4 **2.** $\frac{1}{4}$
3. $1\frac{1}{2}$ and $3\frac{1}{2}$ **4.** $\frac{9}{4}, 2\frac{1}{4}$
5. $\frac{11}{4}$ (or $2\frac{3}{4}$) **6.** $\frac{27}{10}$
7. $1\frac{1}{3}$ $\frac{8}{3}$ **8.** 5
9. $\frac{1}{10} < \frac{1}{7} < \frac{1}{4} < \frac{1}{2}$ **10.** $1\frac{4}{5}, \frac{9}{5}$
11. $\frac{7}{6}$ or $1\frac{1}{6}$ **12.** 9
13. $\frac{7}{9}$ **14.** 20p
15. $\frac{5}{2}, 2\frac{1}{2}$ **16.** $\frac{14}{9}$ or $1\frac{5}{9}$
17. more blue balloons **18.** $1\frac{2}{3}$
19. 84 **20.** <

Page 35
1. $\frac{8}{5}, 1\frac{3}{5}$ **2.** 5
3. 8 **4.** 50p
5. $3\frac{1}{2}$ **6.** more apples
7. < **8.** $\frac{5}{8}$
9. $1\frac{2}{3}, \frac{5}{3}$ **10.** $\frac{9}{8}$ or $1\frac{1}{8}$
11. $\frac{8}{5}$ $2\frac{3}{5}$ **12.** $\frac{4}{7}$
13. 45 **14.** $1\frac{3}{4}, 2\frac{1}{4}$
15. $\frac{1}{10}$ **16.** $\frac{13}{10}$
17. $\frac{1}{8} < \frac{1}{6} < \frac{1}{5} < \frac{1}{3}$ **18.** $\frac{11}{9}$ or $1\frac{2}{9}$
19. $\frac{7}{4}, 1\frac{3}{4}$ **20.** 35

Pages 36–37
1. **a)** 3.4 **b)** 86 **c)** 12.28 **d)** 8.55
   e) 37.2 **f)** 16.2
2. **a)** 368 **b)** 30 **c)** 100.5 **d)** 293.4
   e) 65.5 **f)** 4638.5
3. **a)** 8.35 **b)** 1.9 **c)** 22.76 **d)** 2.845
   e) 0.093 **f)** 1.284
4. **a)** 0.27 **b)** 3.42
   c) 0.538 **d)** 0.063
   e) 0.279 **f)** 1.452
5. 0.855 kg, 0.95 kg, 8.245 kg, 8.3 kg, 8.455 kg, 8.52 kg
6. **a)** 3.3 **b)** 3.8 **c)** 3.1 **d)** 3.6
   e) 3.9 **f)** 3.4

Pages 38–39
1. **a)** 50% **b)** 25% **c)** 10% **d)** 20%
   e) 60% **f)** 72% **g)** 58% **h)** 65%
   i) 80% **j)** 30% **k)** 34% **l)** 55%
2. **a)** $\frac{1}{10}$ **b)** $\frac{4}{5}$ **c)** $\frac{1}{2}$ **d)** $\frac{3}{10}$
   e) $\frac{3}{5}$ **f)** $\frac{1}{4}$ **g)** $\frac{1}{20}$ **h)** $\frac{9}{10}$
   i) $\frac{3}{4}$ **j)** $\frac{2}{5}$ **k)** $\frac{7}{10}$ **l)** $\frac{1}{100}$
3. **a)** 20% **b)** 15% **c)** 35% **d)** 60%
   e) 50% **f)** 30% **g)** 75% **h)** 90%
   i) 85% **j)** 10% **k)** 5% **l)** 70%
4. **a)** 0.3 **b)** 0.45 **c)** 0.65 **d)** 0.8
   e) 0.9 **f)** 0.25 **g)** 0.05 **h)** 0.15
   i) 0.3 **j)** 0.55 **k)** 0.35 **l)** 0.85
5. **a)** 15%, 20%, 25%, $\frac{9}{25}, \frac{6}{10}, \frac{4}{5}$
   b) 10%, $\frac{1}{4}$, 40%, $\frac{23}{50}$, 60%, $\frac{7}{10}$
   c) $\frac{1}{50}$, 3%, $\frac{1}{10}, \frac{3}{20}$, 16%, 50%

Pages 40–41
1. $0.8 \times 3 \rightarrow 2.4$; $2.4 \times 6 \rightarrow 14.4$; $1.4 \times 9 \rightarrow 12.6$;
   $2.3 \times 8 \rightarrow 18.4$; $4.1 \times 5 \rightarrow 20.5$; $0.9 \times 5 \rightarrow 4.5$;
   $1.8 \times 6 \rightarrow 10.8$
2. **a)** 4.5 **b)** 3.6 **c)** 5.6 **d)** 9.2
   e) 7.1 **f)** 10.3
3. **a)** 4.4 **b)** 0.8 **c)** 5.4 **d)** 1.4
   e) 2.5 **f)** 4.8
4. $0.3 \times 6 = 1.8$; $3.4 \times 7 = 23.8$; $1.9 \times 5 = 9.5$; $2.6 \times 4 = 10.4$

Answers

Page 42
1. 50%
2. 13.6
3. 54.32
4. (24%), $\frac{7}{25}$
5. $\frac{3}{10}$
6. 0.8, $\frac{4}{5}$
7. <
8. 0.73
9. 12.8
10. (5.29 kg,) 0.925 kg
11. >
12. 90%
13. 87
14. 4.2, 4 (or 4.0)
15. 2.8
16. 0.12
17. 0.65
18. 6.19
19. 1.5, 1.6
20. 0.5

Page 43
1. $\frac{3}{4}$
2. 1.96
3. 700.4
4. 4.8
5. 2.8, 2.1
6. 1.9
7. 5.7
8. 4.5
9. 45%
10. >
11. (25%), $\frac{7}{20}$
12. 3.8
13. 25%
14. 824
15. 1.093
16. >
17. 11.1
18. (3.05 kg,) 0.532 kg
19. 0.34
20. 0.7

Pages 44–45
1. a) 64   b) 121
   c) 49   d) 36
   e) 81   f) 100
   g) 25   h) 144
2. The square numbers are all in a diagonal line.
3. a) 4   b) 9   c) 16   d) 25
   e) 36   f) 49   g) 64   h) 81
   i) 100
4. They are all square numbers.

Pages 46–47
1. a) 15 cm², 16 cm   b) 24 cm², 20 cm
   c) 25 cm², 20 cm   d) 18 cm², 18 cm
   e) 36 cm², 24 cm   f) 32 cm², 24 cm
2. Area column should be completed as follows:
   36, 40, 48, 49, 40, 45, 52, 100, 54, 121, 64, 400
   Perimeter column should be completed as follows:
   30, 28, 28, 28, 26, 36, 34, 50, 42, 44, 40, 80
3. a) 4 cm   b) 16 cm
4. a) 9 cm   b) 81 cm²

Pages 48–49
1. a) 6.05 p.m.   b) 9.15 a.m.   c) 10.30 a.m.
   d) 3.35 p.m.   e) 8.55 p.m.
2. a) 8.15 a.m.   b) 1 hour 45 minutes (or 1¾ hours)
   c) 4 hours 50 minutes   d) 11.50 a.m.
   e) 6.15 a.m.
3. a) Bus D   b) Bus B

Page 50
1. 16
2. 12 m²
3. 4.05 p.m.
4. Area = 32 cm²; Perimeter = 24 cm
5. 1 hour 25 minutes
6. 7 cm
7. 11.40 a.m.
8. 81
9. 80 cm
10. 10 cm
11. 36
12. 1 hour 40 minutes
13. Area = 27 cm²; Perimeter = 24 cm
14. 6.10 p.m.
15. 144
16. 8 cm
17. 25
18. Saturday
19. 45 minutes
20. Sunday

Page 51
1. Area = 21 cm²; Perimeter = 20 cm
3. 1.15 p.m.
5. 6.55 p.m.
7. 54 m²
9. 1 hour 25 minutes
11. 10 m
13. 6.20 p.m.
15. 121
17. 16
19. 2 hours 10 minutes

2. 49
4. 3 cm
6. 64
8. Sunday
10. Saturday
12. 7.55 a.m.
14. 9 cm
16. 45 minutes
18. Area = 72 cm²; Perimeter = 34 cm
20. 25

Page 52
1. 90
2. 17
3. 20
4. 7
5. 7
6. 21
7. 50
8. 16
9. 50
10. 200
11. 90
12. 23
13. 300
14. $\frac{4}{5}$
15. 140
16. 18
17. 900
18. 0.8
19. 3
20. 15
21. 110
22. 100
23. 13
24. 4
25. 13
26. 20
27. 0.5
28. 4
29. 9
30. 6
31. 90
32. 25
33. $\frac{3}{5}$
34. 15
35. 5
36. 130
37. 22
38. 22
39. 22
40. 60

Page 54
1. 30
2. 32
3. 5
4. 2
5. 18
6. 60
7. 5
8. 5
9. 18
10. 10
11. 20
12. 24
13. 120
14. 4
15. 42
16. 50
17. 11
18. 3
19. 6
20. 27
21. 20
22. 56
23. 99
24. 6
25. 34
26. 55
27. 45
28. 49
29. 16
30. 3
31. 9
32. 240
33. 250
34. 36
35. 12
36. 7
37. 60
38. 48
39. 63
40. 5

Page 56
1. 18
2. 90
3. 36
4. 60
5. 30
6. 40
7. 4
8. 11
9. 24
10. 8
11. 5
12. 48
13. 9
14. 1.2
15. 100
16. 7
17. 32
18. 40
19. 8
20. 40

Answers

21.	48	**22.**	850
23.	60	**24.**	7
25.	16	**26.**	22
27.	60	**28.**	350
29.	15	**30.**	9
31.	6	**32.**	121
33.	5	**34.**	54
35.	4	**36.**	2
37.	32	**38.**	7
39.	14	**40.**	144

Fractions of amounts

2. Complete by writing < or > between each pair of amounts.

   a) $\frac{2}{3}$ of 90 ☐ $\frac{7}{10}$ of 90

   b) $\frac{3}{4}$ of 100 ☐ $\frac{4}{5}$ of 100

   c) $\frac{3}{10}$ of 140 ☐ $\frac{2}{7}$ of 140

   d) $\frac{5}{8}$ of 160 ☐ $\frac{3}{4}$ of 160

3. Answer these.

a) What fraction of £1 is:	b) What fraction of £2 is:	c) What fraction of £10 is:
50p ⟶ ___	20p ⟶ ___	£2.50 ⟶ ___
20p ⟶ ___	£1 ⟶ ___	£5 ⟶ ___
10p ⟶ ___	50p ⟶ ___	£1 ⟶ ___
25p ⟶ ___	£1.50 ⟶ ___	£7.50 ⟶ ___
75p ⟶ ___	40p ⟶ ___	£2 ⟶ ___

4. Read and answer these.

   a) Would it be lighter to carry $\frac{1}{5}$ of 10 kg or $\frac{1}{10}$ of 10 kg?

   _____

   b) Joy wants a large slice of cake. Should she cut the cake into quarters or thirds to get the largest slice?

   _____

   c) There are 24 hours in a day. Peter spends a quarter of the day at school and a third asleep. Does he spend more time at school or more time sleeping?

   _____

   d) There are 45 fish. $\frac{3}{5}$ are spotted and $\frac{2}{9}$ are striped. Are there more striped or more spotted fish?

   _____

Fraction calculations

Learn and revise

Remember that to add and subtract fractions with the same denominator, just add or subtract the numerators.

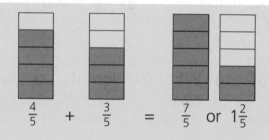

$$\frac{4}{5} \quad + \quad \frac{3}{5} \quad = \quad \frac{7}{5} \quad \text{or} \quad 1\frac{2}{5}$$

$$1\frac{2}{5} - \frac{3}{5} = \underline{\hspace{1cm}}$$

If it is a mixed number, change it to an improper fraction.

$$\frac{7}{5} - \frac{3}{5} = \frac{4}{5}$$

Practice activities

1. Join pairs of fractions that total 3.

$1\frac{3}{4}$	$1\frac{7}{8}$	$1\frac{1}{8}$
$\frac{2}{3}$	$\frac{7}{10}$	
$2\frac{3}{10}$	$1\frac{1}{3}$	$1\frac{2}{3}$
$2\frac{1}{3}$	$1\frac{1}{4}$	

2. Subtract these fractions.

a) $\frac{9}{4} - \frac{1}{4} = \underline{\hspace{1cm}}$

b) $\frac{7}{10} - \frac{1}{10} = \underline{\hspace{1cm}}$

c) $\frac{12}{5} - \frac{3}{5} = \underline{\hspace{1cm}}$

d) $\frac{11}{10} - \frac{3}{10} = \underline{\hspace{1cm}}$

3. Add the shaded parts of these shapes.

a)

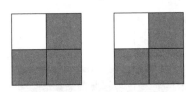

$\frac{3}{4} + \frac{3}{4} =$ _____ or _____

b)

$\frac{5}{6} + \frac{2}{6} =$ _____ or _____

c)

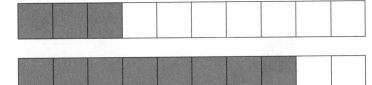

$\frac{3}{10} + \frac{8}{10} =$ _____ or _____

d)

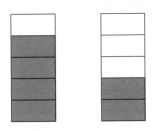

$\frac{4}{5} + \frac{2}{5} =$ _____ or _____

4. Subtract these fractions. Change mixed numbers to improper fractions to make them easier.

a) $1\frac{1}{4} - \frac{3}{4} =$ _____

b) $1\frac{2}{5} - \frac{4}{5} =$ _____

c) $1\frac{3}{10} - \frac{6}{10} =$ _____

d) $1\frac{1}{3} - \frac{2}{3} =$ _____

5. Answer these. Give your answers as fractions or mixed numbers as appropriate.

a) Add together $\frac{1}{4}$ and $6\frac{3}{4}$. _____

b) What is the difference between $1\frac{3}{10}$ m and $\frac{7}{10}$ m? _____ m

c) Total $4\frac{3}{5}$ and $1\frac{3}{5}$. _____

d) How much more is $3\frac{1}{10}$ litres than $\frac{8}{10}$ litres? _____ litres

e) What is the sum of $1\frac{3}{4}$ and $6\frac{3}{4}$? _____

Mental arithmetic test 7

1. $\frac{1}{6}$ of 24 = _____

2. What fraction of £5 is £1.25?

_____

3. Circle **two** fractions that total 5.

$1\frac{1}{2}$ $2\frac{1}{2}$

     $4\frac{1}{2}$ $3\frac{1}{2}$

4. Write this as:

an **improper fraction** _____

a **mixed number** _____

5. $\frac{14}{4} - \frac{3}{4}$ = _____

6. Write $2\frac{7}{10}$ as an improper fraction.

_____

7. Circle the smallest fraction and underline the greatest fraction.

$\frac{7}{3}$ $1\frac{2}{3}$ $\frac{8}{3}$ $1\frac{1}{3}$ $\frac{6}{3}$

8. Add together $\frac{1}{3}$ and $4\frac{2}{3}$.

_____

9. Write these fractions in order.

$\frac{1}{10}$ $\frac{1}{2}$ $\frac{1}{7}$ $\frac{1}{4}$

_____ < _____ < _____ < _____

10. Circle **two** of these with the same value.

$1\frac{4}{5}$ $3\frac{1}{5}$ $\frac{13}{5}$

     $\frac{9}{5}$ $\frac{14}{5}$ $1\frac{3}{5}$

11. Add these and write the answer as an **improper fraction** and a **mixed number**.

$\frac{2}{6} + \frac{5}{6}$ = _____ or _____

12. $\frac{1}{8}$ of 72 = _____

13. $1\frac{2}{9} - \frac{4}{9}$ = _____

14. How much is $\frac{1}{5}$ of £1? _____

15. Write the fraction at the arrow as:

an **improper fraction** _____

a **mixed number** _____

16. Write the answer as an improper fraction and a mixed number.

$\frac{8}{9} + \frac{6}{9}$ = _____ or _____

17. In a bag of 30 balloons, $\frac{3}{10}$ are pink and $\frac{2}{5}$ are blue. Which are there more of, pink or blue balloons?

_____

18. Write $\frac{5}{3}$ as a mixed number. _____

19. $\frac{7}{10}$ of 120 = _____

20. Write < or > to make this true.

$\frac{7}{10}$ of 40 _____ $\frac{4}{5}$ of 40

Score   /20

Mental arithmetic test 8

1. Write this as:

an **improper fraction** _____

a **mixed number** _____

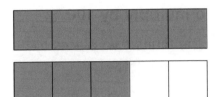

2. $\frac{1}{6}$ of 30 = _____

3. Add together $\frac{1}{2}$ and $7\frac{1}{2}$. _____

4. How much is $\frac{1}{4}$ of £2? _____

5. Write $\frac{7}{2}$ as a mixed number. _____

6. In a box of 21 fruits, $\frac{3}{7}$ are apples and $\frac{1}{3}$ are oranges. Which are there more of, apples or oranges?

_____

7. Write < or > to make this true.

$\frac{3}{4}$ of 60 _____ $\frac{4}{5}$ of 60

8. $\frac{12}{8} - \frac{7}{8} =$ _____

9. Circle **two** of these with the same value.

$2\frac{1}{3}$ $\frac{3}{3}$ $1\frac{2}{3}$

$\frac{5}{3}$ $2\frac{2}{3}$ $\frac{4}{3}$

10. Add these and write the answer as an **improper fraction** and a **mixed number**.

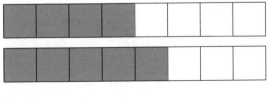

$\frac{4}{8} + \frac{5}{8} =$ _____ or _____

11. Circle the smallest fraction and underline the greatest fraction.

$2\frac{1}{5}$ $\frac{12}{5}$ $2\frac{3}{5}$ $\frac{8}{5}$ $1\frac{4}{5}$

12. $1\frac{2}{7} - \frac{5}{7} =$ _____

13. $\frac{3}{10}$ of 150 = _____

14. Circle **two** fractions that total 4.

$3\frac{1}{4}$ $\frac{1}{4}$ $2\frac{3}{4}$

$1\frac{3}{4}$ $2\frac{1}{4}$

15. What fraction of £5 is 50p? _____

16. Write $1\frac{3}{10}$ as an improper fraction. _____

17. Write these fractions in order.

$\frac{1}{6}$ $\frac{1}{5}$ $\frac{1}{8}$ $\frac{1}{3}$

_____ < _____ < _____ < _____

18. Write the answer as an improper fraction and a mixed number.

$\frac{5}{9} + \frac{6}{9} =$ _____ or _____

19. Write the fraction at the arrow as:

an **improper fraction** _____

a **mixed number** _____

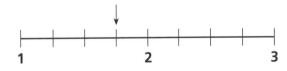

20. $\frac{5}{9}$ of 63 = _____

Decimals

Learn and revise

Follow these rules for multiplying and dividing numbers by 10 and 100.

To multiply by 10

Move the digits one place to the left.

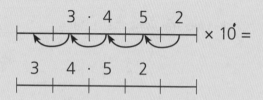

To multiply by 100

Move the digits two places to the left.

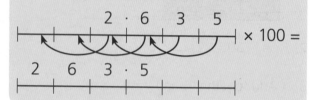

To divide by 10

Move the digits one place to the right.

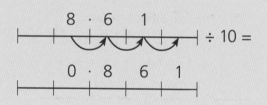

To divide by 100

Move the digits two places to the right.

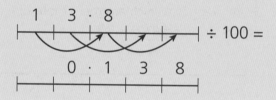

Practice activities

1. Multiply these by 10 and write the answers.

a) 0.34 × 10 = _____

b) 8.6 × 10   = _____

c) 1.228 × 10 = _____

d) 0.855 × 10 = _____

e) 3.72 × 10 = _____

f) 1.62 × 10 = _____

2. Multiply these by 100 and write the answers.

a) 3.68 × 100 = _____

b) 0.3 × 100   = _____

c) 1.005 × 100 = _____

d) 2.934 × 100 = _____

e) 0.655 × 100 = _____

f) 46.385 × 100 = _____

3. Divide these by 10 and write the answers.

a) 83.5 ÷ 10 = _____

b) 19 ÷ 10 = _____

c) 227.6 ÷ 10 = _____

d) 28.45 ÷ 10 = _____

e) 0.93 ÷ 10 = _____

f) 12.84 ÷ 10 = _____

4. Divide these by 100 and write the answers.

a) 27 ÷ 100 = _____

b) 342 ÷ 100 = _____

c) 53.8 ÷ 100 = _____

d) 6.3 ÷ 100 = _____

e) 27.9 ÷ 100 = _____

f) 145.2 ÷ 100 = _____

5. Write these weights in order starting with the lightest.

   8.245 kg   0.95 kg   8.3 kg   0.855 kg

          8.455 kg   8.52 kg

_____

6. Round each decimal number to the nearest tenth. Use the number line to help you.

a) 3.25 _____

b) 3.83 _____

c) 3.08 _____

d) 3.574 _____

e) 3.908 _____

f) 3.445 _____

Fractions, decimals and percentages

Learn and revise

A percentage is a fraction with a denominator of 100.

> To express a fraction as a percentage, change it to an equivalent fraction with a denominator of 100, e.g.
> $$\frac{2}{5} = \frac{40}{100} = 40\%$$

> To express a percentage as a fraction, change it to a fraction with a denominator of 100 and reduce the fraction to its simplest form, e.g.
> $$25\% = \frac{25}{100} = \frac{1}{4}$$

> To express a decimal as a percentage, multiply the decimal by 100, e.g.
> $$0.2 = 20\%$$

> To express a percentage as a decimal, divide the percentage by 100, e.g.
> $$60\% = 0.6$$

Practice activities

1. Write each of these fractions as a percentage.

a) $\frac{1}{2}$ = _____%

b) $\frac{1}{4}$ = _____%

c) $\frac{1}{10}$ = _____%

d) $\frac{1}{5}$ = _____%

e) $\frac{3}{5}$ = _____%

f) $\frac{18}{25}$ = _____%

g) $\frac{29}{50}$ = _____%

h) $\frac{13}{20}$ = _____%

i) $\frac{4}{5}$ = _____%

j) $\frac{3}{10}$ = _____%

k) $\frac{17}{50}$ = _____%

l) $\frac{11}{20}$ = _____%

2. Write each of these percentages as a fraction reduced to its simplest form.

a) 10% = _____

b) 80% = _____

c) 50% = _____

d) 30% = _____

e) 60% = _____

f) 25% = _____

g) 5% = _____

h) 90% = _____

i) 75% = _____

j) 40% = _____

k) 70% = _____

l) 1% = _____

Fractions, decimals and percentages

3. Write each of these decimals as a percentage.

a) 0.2 = ____%

b) 0.15 = ____%

c) 0.35 = ____%

d) 0.6 = ____%

e) 0.5 = ____%

f) 0.3 = ____%

g) 0.75 = ____%

h) 0.9 = ____%

i) 0.85 = ____%

j) 0.1 = ____%

k) 0.05 = ____%

l) 0.7 = ____%

4. Write each of these percentages as a decimal.

a) 30% = _____

b) 45% = _____

c) 65% = _____

d) 80% = _____

e) 90% = _____

f) 25% = _____

g) 5% = _____

h) 15% = _____

i) 30% = _____

j) 55% = _____

k) 35% = _____

l) 85% = _____

5. Order these fractions and percentages from smallest to largest.
You may find it helpful to change all the fractions to percentages.

a)

| $\frac{4}{5}$ | 15% | 25% | $\frac{9}{25}$ | 20% | $\frac{6}{10}$ |

____ ____ ____ ____ ____ ____

smallest

b)

| 40% | $\frac{23}{50}$ | $\frac{1}{4}$ | 10% | $\frac{7}{10}$ | 60% |

____ ____ ____ ____ ____ ____

smallest

c)

| 3% | $\frac{3}{20}$ | 50% | $\frac{1}{10}$ | 16% | $\frac{1}{50}$ |

____ ____ ____ ____ ____ ____

smallest

Decimal calculations

Use facts you know to calculate with decimals. Look at the numbers and decide on the best strategy to work out the answer.

Use near doubles.

Example: What is 3.6 + 3.5?

$$3.5 + 3.5 = 7$$

So 3.5 + 3.6 = 7.1

Count on or back in different jumps.

Example: What is 9.2 − 6.8?

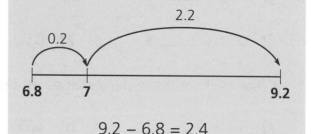

$$9.2 - 6.8 = 2.4$$

Partition, or break numbers up.

Example: What is 4.8 × 5?

$$4 \times 5 = 20$$

$$0.8 \times 5 = 4$$

So 4.8 × 5 = 24

Use facts you know.

Example: What is 0.9 × 7?

$$9 \times 7 = 63$$

So 0.9 × 7 = 6.3

Practice activities

1. Join each of these to the matching answer.

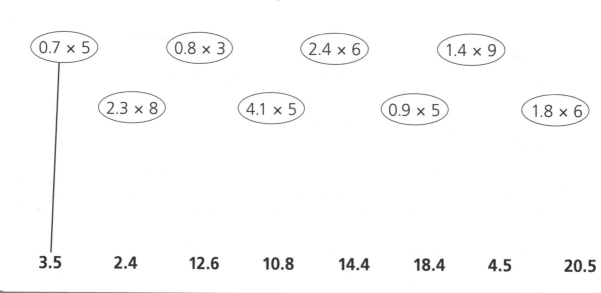

| 0.7 × 5 | 0.8 × 3 | 2.4 × 6 | 1.4 × 9 |

| 2.3 × 8 | 4.1 × 5 | 0.9 × 5 | 1.8 × 6 |

3.5   2.4   12.6   10.8   14.4   18.4   4.5   20.5

2. Answer these.

a) 0.6 + 3.9 = ⎯⎯⎯ **b)** 2.8 + 0.8 = ⎯⎯⎯ **c)** 4.7 + 0.9 = ⎯⎯⎯

d) 6.8 + 2.4 = ⎯⎯⎯ **e)** 5.4 + 1.7 = ⎯⎯⎯ **f)** 7.5 + 2.8 = ⎯⎯⎯

3. Use the number lines to help answer these subtractions.

a) 7.8 − 3.4 = ⎯⎯⎯

0.6

3.4 4   7.8

b) 2.5 − 1.7 = ⎯⎯⎯

1.7   2.5

c) 8.9 − 3.5 = ⎯⎯⎯

3.5   8.9

d) 4.2 − 2.8 = ⎯⎯⎯

2.8   4.2

e) 9.4 − 6.9 = ⎯⎯⎯

6.9   9.4

f) 7.4 − 2.6 = ⎯⎯⎯

2.6   7.4

4. Write the missing digits, 0–5, in these calculations.

| 0 | 1 | 2 | 3 | 4 | 5 |

⬚.⬚ × 6 = 1.8   3.4 × 7 = ⬚3.8

⬚.9 × 5 = 9.⬚   2.6 × 4 = 1 0.⬚

Mental arithmetic test 9

1. $\frac{1}{2} =$ _____%

2. $6.8 \times 2 =$ _____

3. $5.432 \times 10 =$ _____

4. Circle the smallest and underline the largest fraction or percentage in this set.

   $\frac{13}{50}$ 25% $\frac{7}{25}$ 24% $\frac{1}{4}$ 27%

5. Write 30% as a fraction, in its simplest form.

   _____

6. Write the missing digits.

   $80\% = 0.$_____ $= \dfrac{\boxed{}}{5}$

7. Write < or > to make this true.

   4.119 km _____ 4.19 km

8. $73 \div 100 =$ _____

9. $3.2 \times 4 =$ _____

10. Circle the heaviest weight and underline the lightest weight.

    5.2 kg   5.29 kg   2.995 kg

       5.02 kg   0.925 kg

11. Write < or > to make this true.

    30% _____ 0.03

12. $0.9 =$ _____%

13. $0.87 \times 100 =$ _____

14. Round each decimal to the nearest tenth.

    4.17 $\longrightarrow$ _____

    4.017 $\longrightarrow$ _____

15. $4 \times 0.7 =$ _____

16. $12 \div 100 =$ _____

17. Write 65% as a decimal.

    _____

18. $61.9 \div 10 =$ _____

19. Round these to the nearest tenth.

    1.508 $\longrightarrow$ _____

    1.58 $\longrightarrow$ _____

20. Use this number line to help you work out this subtraction.

    |————————————————|
    1.7   2.2

    $2.2 - 1.7 =$ _____

Mental arithmetic test 10

1. Write 75% as a fraction, in its simplest form.

   _____

2. $19.6 \div 10 =$ _____

3. $7.004 \times 100 =$ _____

4. $0.8 \times 6 =$ _____

5. Round these to the nearest tenth.

   $2.83 \longrightarrow$ _____

   $2.083 \longrightarrow$ _____

6. Use this number line to help you work out this subtraction.

   |————————————————————|
   1.8   3.7

   $3.7 - 1.8 =$ _____

7. $0.57 \times 10 =$ _____

8. $3.6 + 0.9 =$ _____

9. $0.45 =$ _____%

10. Write < or > to make this true.

    70% _____ $\frac{3}{5}$

11. Circle the smallest and underline the largest fraction or percentage in this set.

    $\frac{8}{25}$ 25% $\frac{7}{20}$ 30% $\frac{3}{10}$

12. $1.9 \times 2 =$ _____

13. $\frac{1}{4} =$ _____%

14. $8.24 \times 100 =$ _____

15. $109.3 \div 100 =$ _____

16. Write < or > to make this true.

    $6.75\,km$ _____ $6.507\,km$

17. $1.3 + 9.8 =$ _____

18. Circle the heaviest weight and underline the lightest weight.

    $2.03\,kg$ $2.305\,kg$ $3.05\,kg$

    $2.3\,kg$ $0.532\,kg$

19. $34 \div 100 =$ _____

20. Write 70% as a decimal.

    _____

Score   /20

Square numbers

Learn and revise

Look at this pattern.

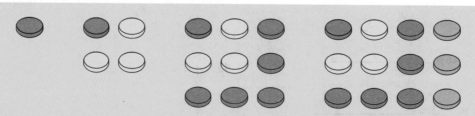

1   4   9   16

The numbers 1, 4, 9 and 16 are examples of **square numbers**, when two identical whole numbers are multiplied together.

1 squared is written as 1^2.

1^2 $\longrightarrow$ $1 \times 1 = 1$

2^2 $\longrightarrow$ $2 \times 2 = 4$

3^2 $\longrightarrow$ $3 \times 3 = 9$

4^2 $\longrightarrow$ $4 \times 4 = 16$

Practice activities

1. Answer these to find more square numbers.

   a) $8^2 =$ _____

   b) $11^2 =$ _____

   c) $7^2 =$ _____

   d) $6^2 =$ _____

   e) $9^2 =$ _____

   f) $10^2 =$ _____

   g) $5^2 =$ _____

   h) $12^2 =$ _____

2. Colour the square numbers on the grid on page 45. What do you notice?

   _____

Square numbers

×	1	2	3	4	5	6	7	8	9	10	11	12
1	1	2	3	4	5	6	7	8	9	10	11	12
2	2	4	6	8	10	12	14	16	18	20	22	24
3	3	6	9	12	15	18	21	24	27	30	33	36
4	4	8	12	16	20	24	28	32	36	40	44	48
5	5	10	15	20	25	30	35	40	45	50	55	60
6	6	12	18	24	30	36	42	48	54	60	66	72
7	7	14	21	28	35	42	49	56	63	70	77	84
8	8	16	24	32	40	48	56	64	72	80	88	96
9	9	18	27	36	45	54	63	72	81	90	99	108
10	10	20	30	40	50	60	70	80	90	100	110	120
11	11	22	33	44	55	66	77	88	99	110	121	132
12	12	24	36	48	60	72	84	96	108	120	132	144

3. Add these consecutive odd numbers and write the total.

a) $1 + 3$ = ____

b) $1 + 3 + 5$ = ____

c) $1 + 3 + 5 + 7$ = ____

d) $1 + 3 + 5 + 7 + 9$ = ____

e) $1 + 3 + 5 + 7 + 9 + 11$ = ____

f) $1 + 3 + 5 + 7 + 9 + 11 + 13$ = ____

g) $1 + 3 + 5 + 7 + 9 + 11 + 13 + 15$ = ____

h) $1 + 3 + 5 + 7 + 9 + 11 + 13 + 15 + 17$ = ____

i) $1 + 3 + 5 + 7 + 9 + 11 + 13 + 15 + 17 + 19$ = ____

4. Look at the answers in practice activity 3. What do you notice about them?

_____

Area and perimeter

Learn and revise

The area of this rectangle is 30 square centimetres or 30 cm². It can be calculated by multiplying the length by the width.

Area = 6 cm × 5 cm = 30 cm²

6 cm

5 cm

> Area of rectangle = Length × Width $A = L \times W$

The perimeter is the distance all the way around a shape. Add together the length of each side of the rectangle.

6 cm + 6 cm + 5 cm + 5 cm = 22 cm

Perimeter = 22 cm

> Perimeter of rectangle = 2 × (Length + Width) $P = 2 \times (L + W)$

Practice activities

1. What are the area and perimeter of each of these?

a)
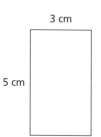
3 cm

5 cm

Area = _____ cm²

Perimeter = _____ cm

b)
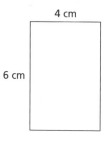
4 cm

6 cm

Area = _____ cm²

Perimeter = _____ cm

c)
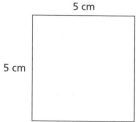
5 cm

5 cm

Area = _____ cm²

Perimeter = _____ cm

d)
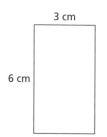
3 cm

6 cm

Area = _____ cm²

Perimeter = _____ cm

e)
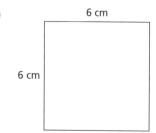
6 cm

6 cm

Area = _____ cm²

Perimeter = _____ cm

f)
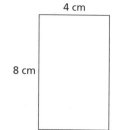
4 cm

8 cm

Area = _____ cm²

Perimeter = _____ cm

2. This table shows the length and width of different rectangles.

Complete the table.

Length (L)	Width (W)	Area (cm²) L × W	Perimeter (cm) 2 × (L + W)
12 cm	3 cm		
4 cm	10 cm		
6 cm	8 cm		
7 cm	7 cm		
5 cm	8 cm		
15 cm	3 cm		
4 cm	13 cm		
20 cm	5 cm		
18 cm	3 cm		
11 cm	11 cm		
16 cm	4 cm		
20 cm	20 cm		

3. The area of a square is 16 cm².

a) What is the length of each side? _____ cm

b) What is the perimeter of the square? _____ cm

4. The perimeter of a square is 36 cm.

a) What is the length of each side? _____ cm

b) What is the area of the square? _____ cm²

Time

Learn and revise

The duration of an event is how much time it takes. A timeline is very useful to help work this out.

Example:

A film starts at 6.40 p.m. and finishes at 8.15 p.m. How long does the film last?

Use a timeline and count on from the start to the finish:

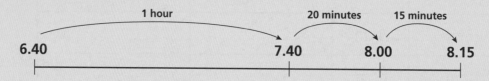

	1 hour		20 minutes	15 minutes
6.40		7.40	8.00	8.15

1 hour + 20 minutes + 15 minutes is 1 hour 35 minutes.

So the film lasts for 1 hour 35 minutes.

Practice activities

1. Write the time that is:

   a) 40 minutes later than 5.25 p.m. _____

   b) 25 minutes later than 8.50 a.m. _____

   c) 20 minutes earlier than 10.50 a.m. _____

   d) 45 minutes earlier than 4.20 p.m. _____

   e) 1 hour 10 minutes later than 7.45 p.m. _____

2. Answer these.

a) It takes Ben 35 minutes to walk to school.

If he arrives at 8.50 a.m., at what time does he leave home? _____

b) Jim drove a lorry from 6.55 a.m. until 8.40 a.m. before taking a rest.

How long had he been driving for? _____

c) A market stall opens at 8.15 a.m. and closes at 1.05 p.m.

How long is the stall open for? _____

d) David ran a half-marathon and finished in 1 hour 35 minutes.

If the race started at 10.15 a.m., what time did he finish? _____

e) Alice falls asleep at 8.50 p.m. and sleeps for 9 hours 25 minutes.

What time does she wake up? _____

3. Look at this bus timetable.

	Bus A	Bus B	Bus C	Bus D
School	8.15 a.m.	9.35 a.m.	11.05 a.m.	1.55 p.m.
Hospital	8.35 a.m.	9.50 a.m.	11.30 a.m.	2.15 p.m.
Market	8.45 a.m.	10.00 a.m.	11.40 a.m.	2.35 p.m.
Town Centre	9.10 a.m.	10.30 a.m.	12.05 p.m.	2.45 p.m.

a) Which is the fastest bus from the school to the town centre?

_____

b) Which is the slowest bus from the hospital to the town centre?

_____

Mental arithmetic test 11

1. $4^2 =$ _____

2. What is the area of a room in the shape of a rectangle with sides 3 m wide and 4 m long?

    _____ m²

3. What time is 45 minutes later than 3.20 p.m.?

    _____

4.

    | 8 cm |

    4 cm

    Area   = _____ cm²

    Perimeter = _____ cm

5. A film starts at 7.15 p.m. and finishes at 8.40 p.m. How long is the film?

    _____

6. The perimeter of a square is 28 cm. What is the length of each side?

    _____ cm

7. Shobna's dance class starts at 10.10 a.m. and lasts for 1 hour 30 minutes. What time does the dance class finish?

    _____

8. $9^2 =$ _____

9. What is the perimeter of a photo frame in the shape of a rectangle with sides 15 cm wide and 25 cm long?

    _____ cm

10. The area of a square is 100 cm². What is the length of each side?

    _____ cm

11. Circle the square number.

    48   55

    36   60

12. How long is 55 minutes and 45 minutes in total?

    _____

13.

    9 cm

    3 cm

    Area   = _____ cm²

    Perimeter = _____ cm

14. A bus leaves at 5.30 p.m., drives 15 minutes to the doctor's and drives another 25 minutes to the bus station. What time does it arrive at the bus station?

    _____

15. $12^2 =$ _____

16. The area of a square is 64 cm². What is the length of each side?

    _____ cm

17. What is the next square number?

    4   9   16   _____

    These are the times of a TV show Maths Fun! Use this information in 18–20.

Maths Fun!	Saturday	Sunday
Starts	11.40 a.m.	4.55 p.m.
Finishes	12.25 p.m.	6.10 p.m.

18. On which day is Maths Fun! on TV in the morning?

    _____

19. How long is the Saturday Maths Fun! show?

    _____

20. Which is the longest Maths Fun! show, Saturday or Sunday?

    _____

Score   /20

50

Mental arithmetic test 12

1.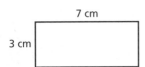

   7 cm

   3 cm

   Area   = _____ cm²

   Perimeter = _____ cm

2. 7^2 = _____

3. A shop closes at 12.30 p.m. for 45 minutes for lunch. What time does the shop re-open after lunch?

   _____

4. The perimeter of a square is 12 cm. What is the length of each side?

   _____ cm

5. What time is 20 minutes before 7.15 p.m.?

   _____

6. 8^2 = _____

7. What is the area of a garden in the shape of a rectangle 6 m wide and 9 m long?

   _____ m²

   Use these swimming times in 8–10.

Swim Class	Saturday	Sunday
Starts	10.35 a.m.	11.20 a.m.
Finishes	11.50 a.m.	12.45 p.m.

8. Jo wants a class that starts as late as possible. Which class is at the later time, Saturday or Sunday?

   _____

9. How long is Sunday's class?

   _____

10. Which is the shorter swimming class, Saturday or Sunday?

    _____

11. What is the perimeter of a pond in the shape of a rectangle 2 m wide and 3 m long?

    _____ m

12. I wake at 7.30 a.m. I take 15 minutes to dress and 10 minutes to eat breakfast, then I am ready. At what time am I ready?

    _____

13. What time is 1 hour 30 minutes later than 4.50 p.m.?

    _____

14. The area of a square is 81 cm². What is the length of each side?

    _____ cm

15. 11^2 = _____

16. Class B's Maths lesson starts at 9.55 a.m. and ends at 10.40 a.m. How long is Class B's Maths lesson?

    _____ minutes

17. What is the next square number?

    1   4   9   _____

18.

    8 cm

    9 cm

    Area   = _____ cm²

    Perimeter = _____ cm

19. How long is 1 hour 20 minutes and 50 minutes altogether?

    _____

20. Circle the square number.

    30   44

         18   25

Score   /20

51

Speed test

- How many of these can you complete correctly in one minute?
- Write your answers on paper. Number them 1 to 40.
- Don't worry if you cannot answer them all, just answer them as quickly as you can.
- Stop after one minute, check your answers and record your score on the progress chart opposite.
- Then, try again at another time to see if you can improve your score!

Addition and subtraction

1. 20 + 70 = _____

2. 9 + 8 = _____

3. 13 + 7 = _____

4. 16 − 9 = _____

5. 20 − 13 = _____

6. 15 + 6 = _____

7. 80 − 30 = _____

8. 9 + 7 = _____

9. 100 − 50 = _____

10. 800 − 600 = _____

11. 120 − 30 = _____

12. 15 + 8 = _____

13. 150 + 150 = _____

14. $\frac{2}{5} + \frac{2}{5}$ = _____

15. 70 + 70 = _____

16. 21 − 3 = _____

17. 400 + 500 = _____

18. 0.5 + 0.3 = _____

19. 12 − 9 = _____

20. 7 + 8 = _____

21. 20 + 90 = _____

22. 60 + 40 = _____

23. 19 − 6 = _____

24. 11 − 7 = _____

25. 6 + 7 = _____

26. 110 − 90 = _____

27. 0.8 − 0.3 = _____

28. 16 − 12 = _____

29. 13 − 4 = _____

30. 17 − 11 = _____

31. 50 + 40 = _____

32. 17 + 8 = _____

33. $\frac{4}{5} − \frac{1}{5}$ = _____

34. 9 + 6 = _____

35. 13 − 8 = _____

36. 80 + 50 = _____

37. 18 + 4 = _____

38. 27 − 5 = _____

39. 16 + 6 = _____

40. 100 − 40 = _____

Progress chart

Colour in the stars to show your correct answers.

Attempt	1	2	3	4	5	6
Date	....	....	....	....	....	....

Scores out of 40

Column 1: 39 40 / 37 38 / 35 36 / 33 34 / 31 32 / 29 30 / 27 28 / 25 26 / 23 24 / 21 22 / 19 20 / 17 18 / 15 16 / 13 14 / 11 12 / 9 10 / 7 8 / 5 6 / 3 4 / 1 2

Column 2: 39 40 / 37 38 / 35 36 / 33 34 / 31 32 / 29 30 / 27 28 / 25 26 / 23 24 / 21 22 / 19 20 / 17 18 / 15 16 / 13 14 / 11 12 / 9 10 / 7 8 / 5 6 / 3 4 / 1 2

Column 3: 39 40 / 37 38 / 35 36 / 33 34 / 31 32 / 29 30 / 27 28 / 25 26 / 23 24 / 21 22 / 19 20 / 17 18 / 15 16 / 13 14 / 11 12 / 9 10 / 7 8 / 5 6 / 3 4 / 1 2

Column 4: 39 40 / 37 38 / 35 36 / 33 34 / 31 32 / 29 30 / 27 28 / 25 26 / 23 24 / 21 22 / 19 20 / 17 18 / 15 16 / 13 14 / 11 12 / 9 10 / 7 8 / 5 6 / 3 4 / 1 2

Column 5: 39 40 / 37 38 / 35 36 / 33 34 / 31 32 / 29 30 / 27 28 / 25 26 / 23 24 / 21 22 / 19 20 / 17 18 / 15 16 / 13 14 / 11 12 / 9 10 / 7 8 / 5 6 / 3 4 / 1 2

Column 6: 39 40 / 37 38 / 35 36 / 33 34 / 31 32 / 29 30 / 27 28 / 25 26 / 23 24 / 21 22 / 19 20 / 17 18 / 15 16 / 13 14 / 11 12 / 9 10 / 7 8 / 5 6 / 3 4 / 1 2

Speed test

- How many of these can you complete correctly in one minute?
- Write your answers on paper. Number them 1 to 40.
- Don't worry if you cannot answer them all, just answer them as quickly as you can.
- Stop after one minute, check your answers and record your score on the progress chart opposite.
- Then, try again at another time to see if you can improve your score!

Multiplication and division

1. 6 × 5 = _____

2. 8 × 4 = _____

3. 55 ÷ 11 = _____

4. 16 ÷ 8 = _____

5. 6 × 3 = _____

6. 12 × 5 = _____

7. 30 ÷ 6 = _____

8. 15 ÷ 3 = _____

9. 9 × 2 = _____

10. 90 ÷ 9 = _____

11. 80 ÷ 4 = _____

12. 4 × 6 = _____

13. 12 × 10 = _____

14. 32 ÷ 8 = _____

15. 6 × 7 = _____

16. 5 × 10 = _____

17. 110 ÷ 10 = _____

18. 21 ÷ 7 = _____

19. 36 ÷ 6 = _____

20. 3 × 9 = _____

21. 40 ÷ 2 = _____

22. 8 × 7 = _____

23. 9 × 11 = _____

24. 18 ÷ 3 = _____

25. 3.4 × 10 = _____

26. 11 × 5 = _____

27. 5 × 9 = _____

28. 7 × 7 = _____

29. 160 ÷ 10 = _____

30. 24 ÷ 8 = _____

31. 54 ÷ 6 = _____

32. 40 × 6 = _____

33. 25 × 10 = _____

34. 6 × 6 = _____

35. 120 ÷ 10 = _____

36. 28 ÷ 4 = _____

37. 2 × 30 = _____

38. 8 × 6 = _____

39. 9 × 7 = _____

40. 25 ÷ 5 = _____

Progress chart

Colour in the stars to show your correct answers.

Attempt	1	2	3	4	5	6
Date	....	....	....	....	....	....

Scores out of 40

1	2	3	4	5	6
39 40	39 40	39 40	39 40	39 40	39 40
37 38	37 38	37 38	37 38	37 38	37 38
35 36	35 36	35 36	35 36	35 36	35 36
33 34	33 34	33 34	33 34	33 34	33 34
31 32	31 32	31 32	31 32	31 32	31 32
29 30	29 30	29 30	29 30	29 30	29 30
27 28	27 28	27 28	27 28	27 28	27 28
25 26	25 26	25 26	25 26	25 26	25 26
23 24	23 24	23 24	23 24	23 24	23 24
21 22	21 22	21 22	21 22	21 22	21 22
19 20	19 20	19 20	19 20	19 20	19 20
17 18	17 18	17 18	17 18	17 18	17 18
15 16	15 16	15 16	15 16	15 16	15 16
13 14	13 14	13 14	13 14	13 14	13 14
11 12	11 12	11 12	11 12	11 12	11 12
9 10	9 10	9 10	9 10	9 10	9 10
7 8	7 8	7 8	7 8	7 8	7 8
5 6	5 6	5 6	5 6	5 6	5 6
3 4	3 4	3 4	3 4	3 4	3 4
1 2	1 2	1 2	1 2	1 2	1 2

Speed test

- How many of these can you complete correctly in one minute?
- Write your answers on paper. Number them 1 to 40.
- Don't worry if you cannot answer them all, just answer them as quickly as you can.
- Stop after one minute, check your answers and record your score on the progress chart opposite.
- Then, try again at another time to see if you can improve your score!

Mixed problems

1. 9 + 9 = _____

2. 30 + 60 = _____

3. 9 × 4 = _____

4. 90 – 30 = _____

5. 60 ÷ 2 = _____

6. 90 – 50 = _____

7. 36 ÷ 9 = _____

8. 7 + 4 = _____

9. 3 × 8 = _____

10. 88 ÷ 11 = _____

11. 12 – 7 = _____

12. 12 × 4 = _____

13. 15 – 6 = _____

14. 0.6 + 0.6 = _____

15. 50 + 50 = _____

16. 35 ÷ 5 = _____

17. 4 × 8 = _____

18. 70 – 30 = _____

19. 32 ÷ 4 = _____

20. 8 × 5 = _____

21. 6 × 8 = _____

22. 650 + 200 = _____

23. 180 ÷ 3 = _____

24. 12 – 5 = _____

25. 4 × 4 = _____

26. 19 + 3 = _____

27. 80 – 20 = _____

28. 70 × 5 = _____

29. 7 + 8 = _____

30. 18 – 9 = _____

31. 36 ÷ 6 = _____

32. 11 × 11 = _____

33. 13 – 8 = _____

34. 9 × 6 = _____

35. 28 ÷ 7 = _____

36. 12 ÷ 6 = _____

37. 8 × 4 = _____

38. 15 – 8 = _____

39. 9 + 5 = _____

40. 12 × 12 = _____

Progress chart

Colour in the stars to show your correct answers.

	Attempt 1	Attempt 2	Attempt 3	Attempt 4	Attempt 5	Attempt 6

Date ....

Scores out of 40

39 40	39 40	39 40	39 40	39 40	39 40
37 38	37 38	37 38	37 38	37 38	37 38
35 36	35 36	35 36	35 36	35 36	35 36
33 34	33 34	33 34	33 34	33 34	33 34
31 32	31 32	31 32	31 32	31 32	31 32
29 30	29 30	29 30	29 30	29 30	29 30
27 28	27 28	27 28	27 28	27 28	27 28
25 26	25 26	25 26	25 26	25 26	25 26
23 24	23 24	23 24	23 24	23 24	23 24
21 22	21 22	21 22	21 22	21 22	21 22
19 20	19 20	19 20	19 20	19 20	19 20
17 18	17 18	17 18	17 18	17 18	17 18
15 16	15 16	15 16	15 16	15 16	15 16
13 14	13 14	13 14	13 14	13 14	13 14
11 12	11 12	11 12	11 12	11 12	11 12
9 10	9 10	9 10	9 10	9 10	9 10
7 8	7 8	7 8	7 8	7 8	7 8
5 6	5 6	5 6	5 6	5 6	5 6
3 4	3 4	3 4	3 4	3 4	3 4
1 2	1 2	1 2	1 2	1 2	1 2

Key facts

×	1	2	3	4	5	6	7	8	9	10	11	12
1	1	2	3	4	5	6	7	8	9	10	11	12
2	2	4	6	8	10	12	14	16	18	20	22	24
3	3	6	9	12	15	18	21	24	27	30	33	36
4	4	8	12	16	20	24	28	32	36	40	44	48
5	5	10	15	20	25	30	35	40	45	50	55	60
6	6	12	18	24	30	36	42	48	54	60	66	72
7	7	14	21	28	35	42	49	56	63	70	77	84
8	8	16	24	32	40	48	56	64	72	80	88	96
9	9	18	27	36	45	54	63	72	81	90	99	108
10	10	20	30	40	50	60	70	80	90	100	110	120
11	11	22	33	44	55	66	77	88	99	110	121	132
12	12	24	36	48	60	72	84	96	108	120	132	144

Fractions, decimals and percentages

$\frac{1}{2} = 0.5 = 50\%$	$\frac{1}{4} = 0.25 = 25\%$	$\frac{3}{4} = 0.75 = 75\%$
$\frac{1}{5} = 0.2 = 20\%$	$\frac{1}{10} = 0.1 = 10\%$	$\frac{2}{5} = 0.4 = 40\%$

A fraction has two parts:

$\dfrac{2}{3}$ ⟵ **numerator**
⟵ **denominator**

A **proper fraction** is less than 1. The numerator is smaller than the denominator, e.g. $\frac{3}{5}$	An **improper fraction** is greater than 1. The numerator is greater than the denominator, e.g. $\frac{5}{3}$	A **mixed number** is made up of a whole number and a fraction. $\frac{5}{3} = 1\frac{2}{3}$

Key facts

Multiples

A multiple of a whole number is produced by multiplying that number by another whole number.

Multiples of 3 ⟶ 3 6 9 **12** 15 18… 60… 300…

Multiples of 4 ⟶ 4 8 **12** 16 20 24… 80… 400…

12 is a **common multiple** of both 3 and 4.

Factors

The factors of 8 are **1**, **2**, **4** and **8**.

The factors of 24 are **1**, **2**, 3, **4**, 6, **8**, 12 and 24.

The factors of 32 are **1**, **2**, **4**, **8**, 16 and 32.

The **common factors** of 8, 24 and 32 are 1, 2, 4 and 8.

Measures

Length	Capacity	Weight/Mass
1 kilometre (km) = 1000 metres (m)	1 litre (l) = 1000 millilitres (ml)	1 kilogram (kg) = 1000 grams (g)
1 metre (m) = 100 centimetres (cm)	1 litre (l) = 100 centilitres (cl)	
1 centimetre (cm) = 10 millimetres (mm)		

Time

1 minute = 60 seconds

1 hour = 60 minutes

1 day = 24 hours

1 week = 7 days

1 fortnight = 14 days

1 year = 12 months = 365 days

leap year = 366 days

Acknowledgements

The author and publisher are grateful to the copyright holders for permission to use quoted materials and images.

Cover, P01 ©Igorrita; P16 ©Matthew Cole; P16 © Bernil; P17 ©Natali Snailcat; P28 ©Matthew Cole; P30 ©Matthew Cole; P30 ©Emeric; P31 ©Rinslet; P49 ©Paul Kooi; P52, 54, 56 ©Elmm

The above images have been used under license from Shutterstock.com

All other images are © Letts Educational, an imprint of HarperCollins*Publishers* Ltd

Published by Letts Educational
An imprint of HarperCollins*Publishers* Ltd
1 London Bridge Street
London SE1 9GF

ISBN 9780008294137

First published 2013

This edition published 2018

10 9 8 7 6 5 4 3 2 1

Text © 2018 Paul Broadbent

Design © 2018 Letts Educational, an imprint of HarperCollins*Publishers* Ltd

British Library Cataloguing in Publication Data.

A CIP record of this book is available from the British Library.

Commissioning Editor: Tammy Poggo

Author: Paul Broadbent

Project Manager: Richard Toms

Editorial: Amanda Dickson, Richard Toms and Marie Taylor

Cover Design: Paul Oates

Inside Concept Design: Ian Wrigley

Layout: Jouve India Private Limited

Production: Natalia Rebow

Printed by Bell and Bain Ltd, Glasgow

MIX
Paper from
responsible sources
FSC
www.fsc.org   FSC™ C007454